MW01632572

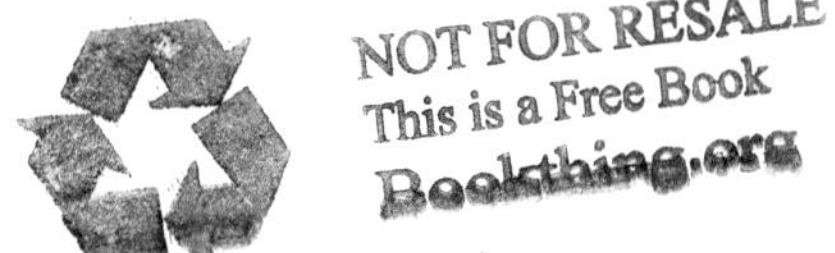
NOT FOR RESALE
This is a Free Book
Bookthing.org

IS SHE AN ARAB

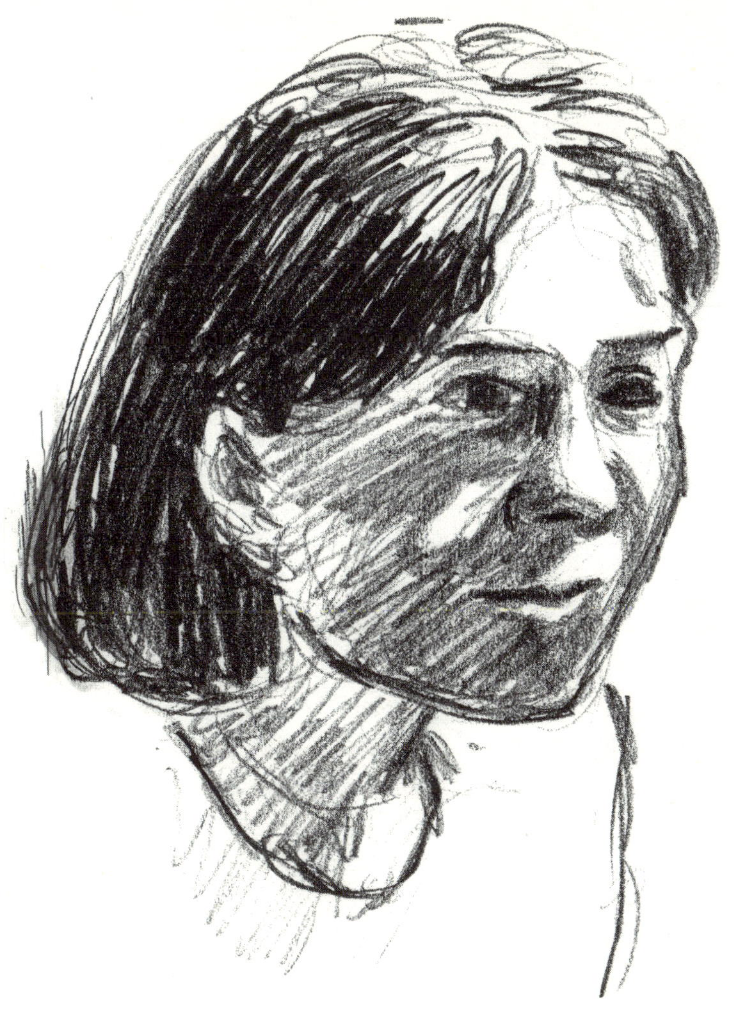

OR A JEW?

PORTRAITS OF ISRAELIS AND PALESTINIANS

FOR MY PARENTS

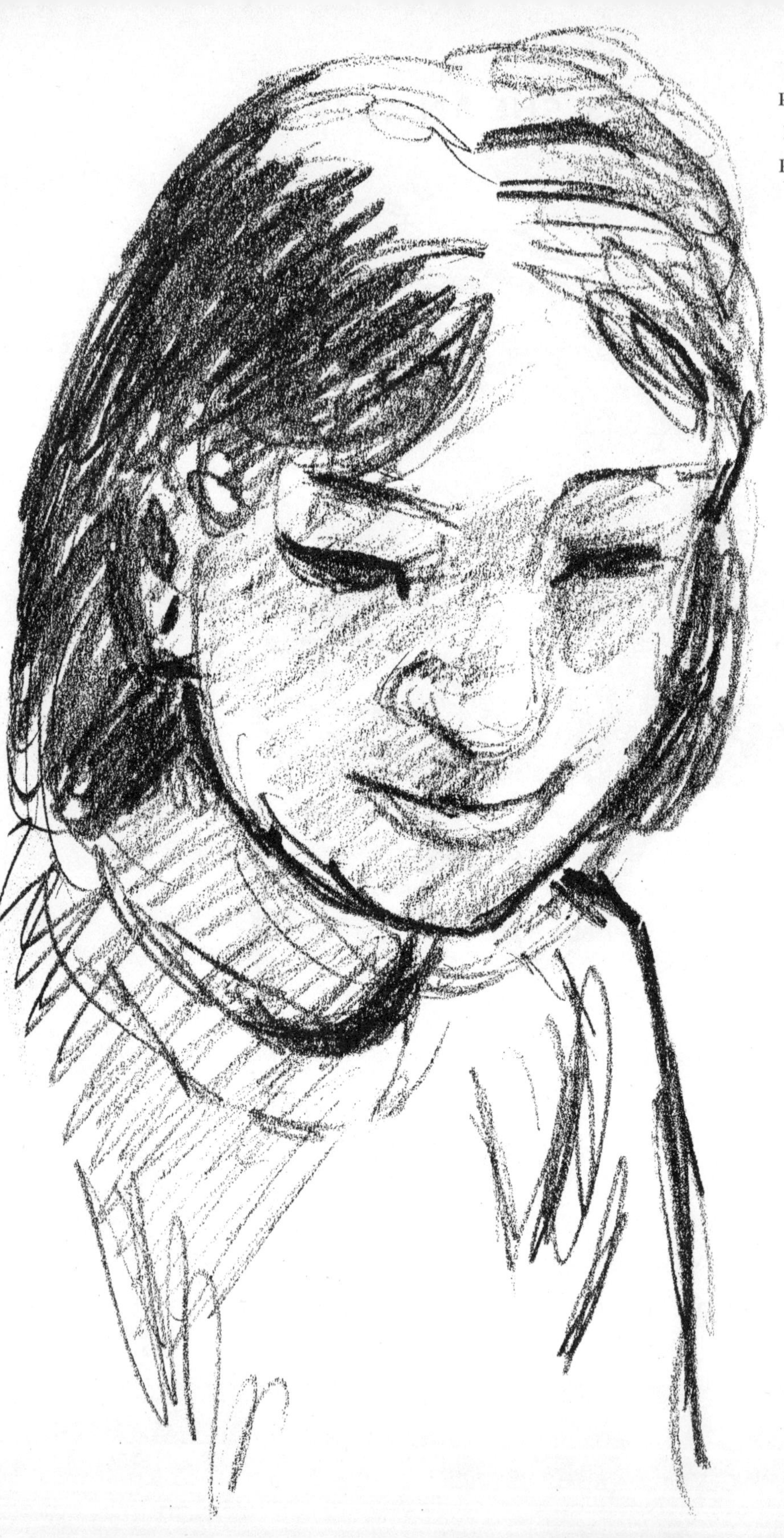

PORTRAITS
ISRAELIS AN
PALESTINIAN

FOR M
PAREN

B
SET
TOBOCMA

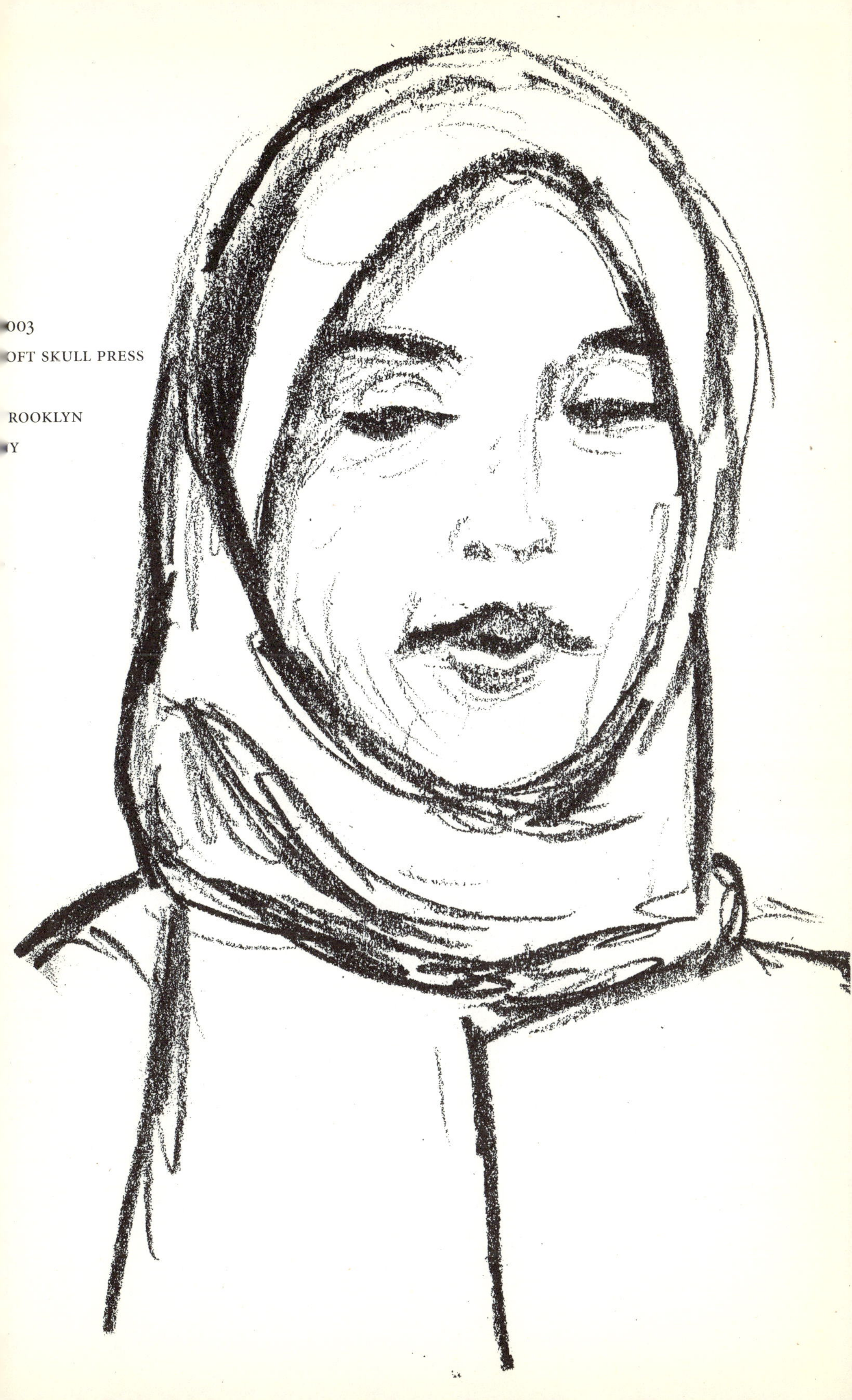

003
OFT SKULL PRESS
ROOKLYN
Y

Portraits of Israelis and Palestinians: For My Parents
ISBN: 1-887128-83-2

First Edition, April 2003

Editorial: Richard Nash
Book Design: David Janik, Amanda Luker

Distributed by Publishers Group West
www.pgw.com | 800.788.3123

Printed in Canada

Soft Skull Press
71 Bond Street
Brooklyn, NY 11217
www.softskull.com

Table of Contents

INTRODUCTION
by Eric Drooker

Needless to say, the entire subject of Israel and the Palestinians is an emotionally explosive issue for Jewish Americans. During a family dinner, for instance, if a beloved son or daughter were to sincerely question, for an instant, the fundamental precepts of Zionism — STAND BACK!! — *Sparks will fly*...and no one will remain unscathed. Not only does everyone have a strong opinion on the subject, but everyone seems to be an expert—whether or not they have ever been to the Middle East. I'm reminded of my grandfather, who frequently pointed out, "If five Jews are arguing with each other — they'll wind up having *six* different opinions."

After the second Palestinian uprising, or "intifada," was sparked in September 2000, Seth Tobocman began drawing and painting images which dramatized the peculiar nature of the conflict. Here was a conflict at once alien, yet strangely familiar. A colonial conflict that, in certain ways, mirrored his own experiences living in the disputed territory of Manhattan's Lower East Side.

In his graphic novel, *War in the Neighborhood*, Seth recounted his years as an eyewitness — as well as participant — in the local, urban upheavals which transformed his low-income neighborhood into an economic combat zone between real estate investors and community residents. In a few short years, thousands of families were uprooted from their homes and relocated elsewhere . . . only to be replaced by younger, wealthier, fairer-skinned inhabitants.

The wholesale displacement of Palestinian communities living under Israeli military occupation is, of course, on a vastly greater scale than the gentrification which occurs on the Lower East Side of New York City. Its methods are far more brutal. In order to make a suitable comparison, one would need to travel back in time to the original displacement of Manhattan Island, or at least as far back as the colonial doctrine of *Manifest Destiny*, enacted on the native inhabitants of America's western frontier.

That the Jewish People were victims of mass-genocide in 20th Century Europe is undeniable, as is the historical fact that their ancestral roots are in the Middle East. These two facts certainly add layers of complexity to the current situation.

For many years, since the *first* intifada, Seth felt deeply unsatisfied with the biased news he received from the mainstream media. Even those few alternative channels on the left irritated him. So he finally decided to visit Palestine, for a month, and see with his own eyes what was up.

It occurred to him that if his parents in Florida knew just where he was going, they would surely flip out. So he told them he was going to Italy. (When he presented this book to them as a gift, his parents thanked him for concealing his true whereabouts. "*We would have been pulling our hair out daily*", they admitted.)

Seth arrived in the Mideast in June 2002, and spent several weeks exploring various parts of Israel and Palestine. Seth's travel in the West Bank was arranged by the International Solidarity Movement, a Palestinian-led organization of activists from around the world, working to raise awareness of the struggle for Palestinian freedom, and an end to the Israeli occupation.

In the West Bank village of Dir Ibzia is a summer school where Seth offered his creative skills, for a couple of weeks, as a teacher. He spent long hours drawing with, and giving artistic advice to the village children. (The first time I ever met Seth, back in 1984, was at a makeshift afterschool art program, on the Lower East Side, where we both volunteered.)

Wherever Seth found himself, he recorded his impressions in his sketchbook, making quick notes of those details which struck him as oddly significant. You hold in your hands a collection of portraits—drawn on the fly—at a critical moment in history. Here are some faces of individuals who, from time immemorial, have been portrayed as faceless, nameless . . . *invisible.*

—March 13, 2003

AUTHOR'S NOTE

by Seth Tobocman

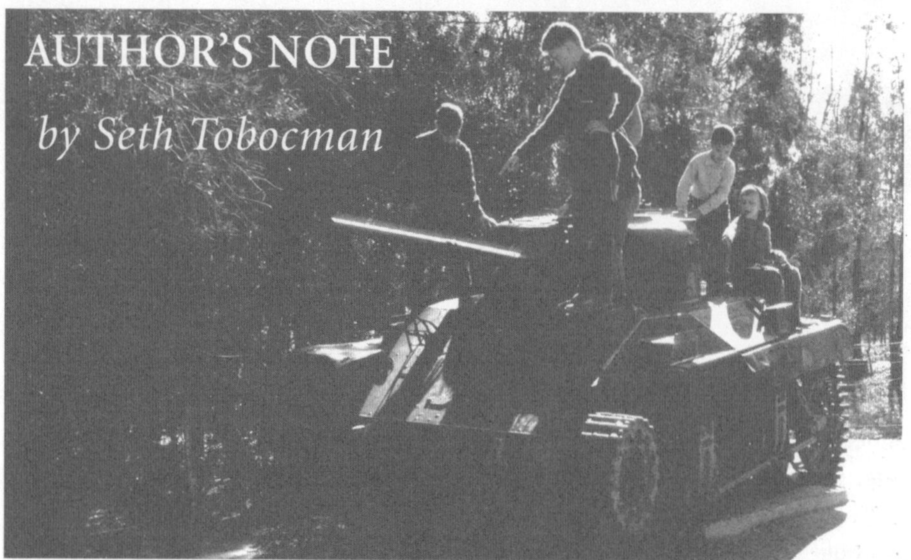

Seth Tobocman with his father and other children atop a tank in Israel, early 1960s

I am an American Jew born in 1958. I grew up in Cleveland, but like many American Jews, I spent a year in Israel. I was three years old at the time.

My parents are wonderful people who taught me to work hard and to stay away from alcohol and cigarettes. They were not religious but they were Zionists and we had a Zionist education in our home. I knew about the Nazi Holocaust before I could sign my name, knew the significance of numbers tattooed on a man's arm before I could add and subtract. And I believed that Israel was our salvation.

I did not question this belief until going to college. There I met a lot of Arab students and I had to deal with the fact that what was a good thing for us was not necessarily a good thing for them.

As an adult I became a political cartoonist. My work has dealt with many issues but only rarely with Israel. Generally, I took the approach of many Jewish radicals of my generation, to let sleeping dogs lie.

But recently I have been working with a lot of younger people, in the Anti-globalization movement. A lot of them, Jews and Gentiles alike, made the brave decision to go to Israel and work for justice and peace there. And it was this that inspired me to go there and see the situation for myself.

These are some of the sketches I made traveling around the area, with some commentary by the artist. I don't claim to be an expert on the Middle East. I am neither an Israeli nor a Palestinian. But in many ways, the fate of that region has been in the hands of Americans who aren't experts, Americans like you and me. That's why it's important for us to come to a better understanding of the situation. I hope we make the right decisions.

A LAND WITH 2 PEOPLES

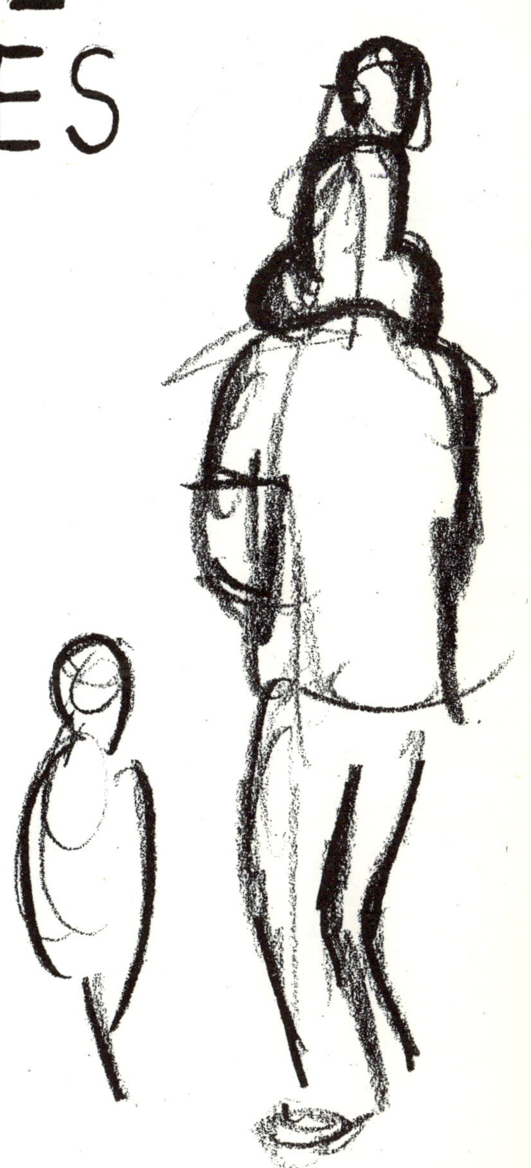

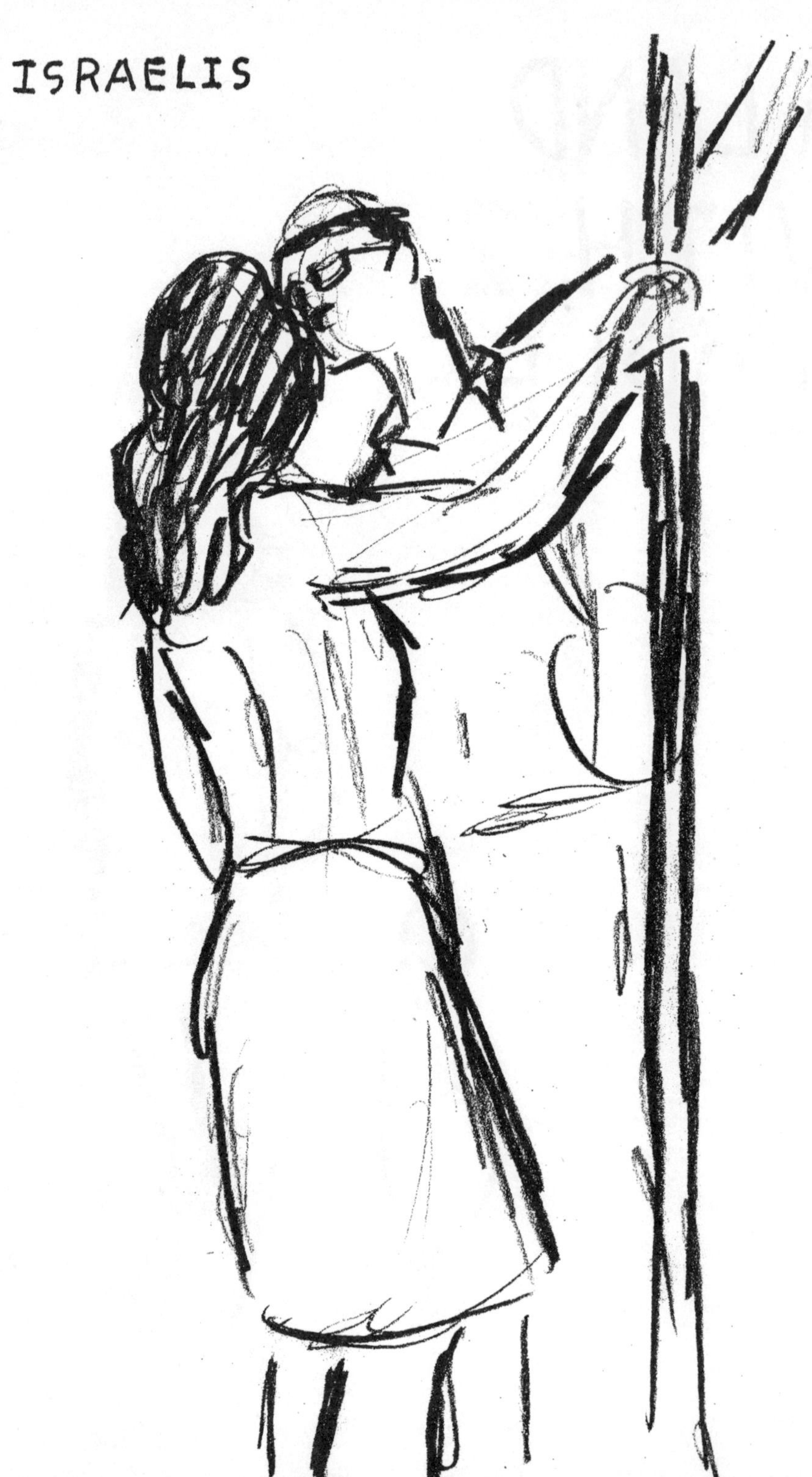
ISRAELIS

THEY ARE GETTING ON A PLANE AND GOING TO ISRAEL.

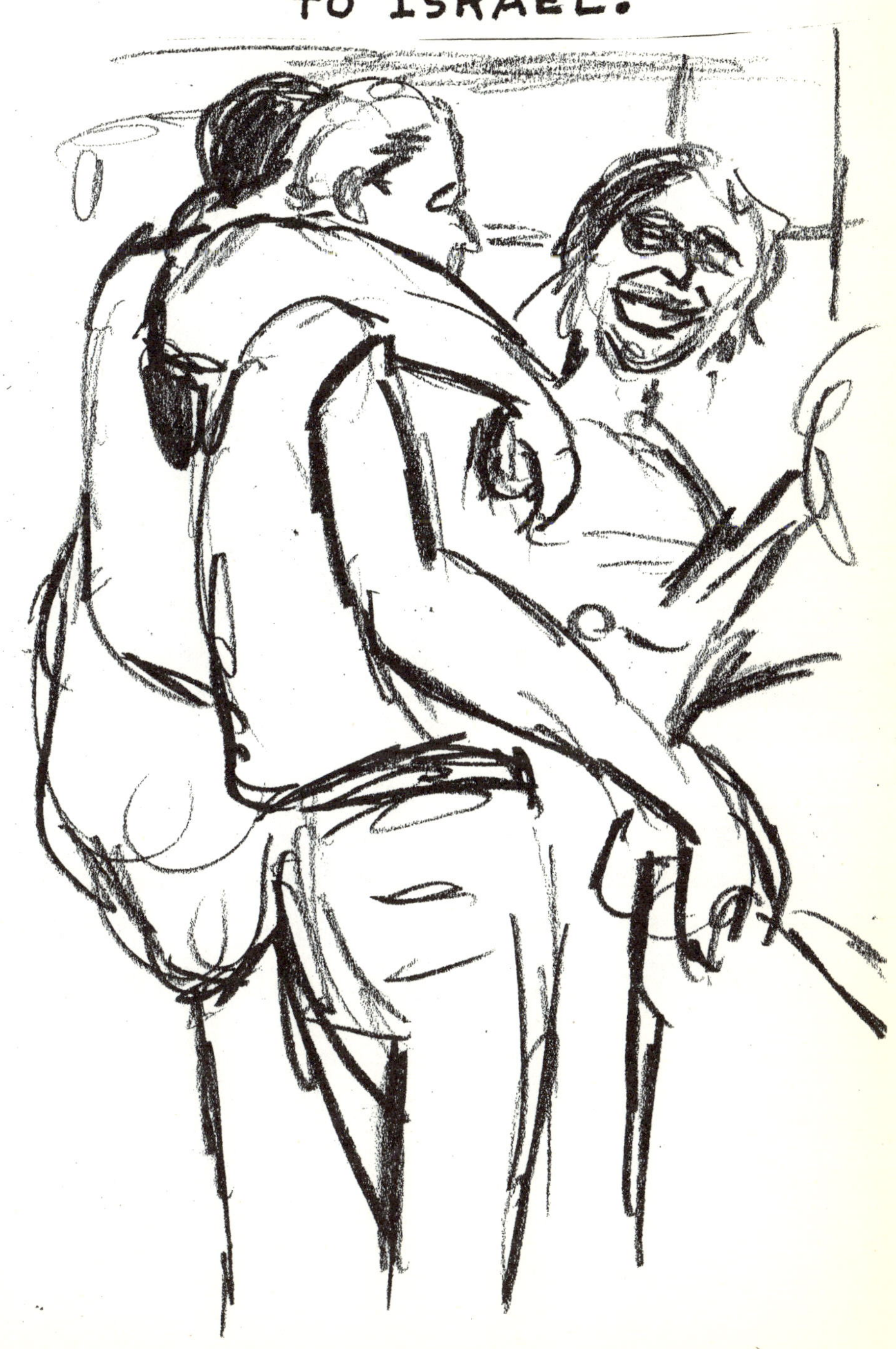

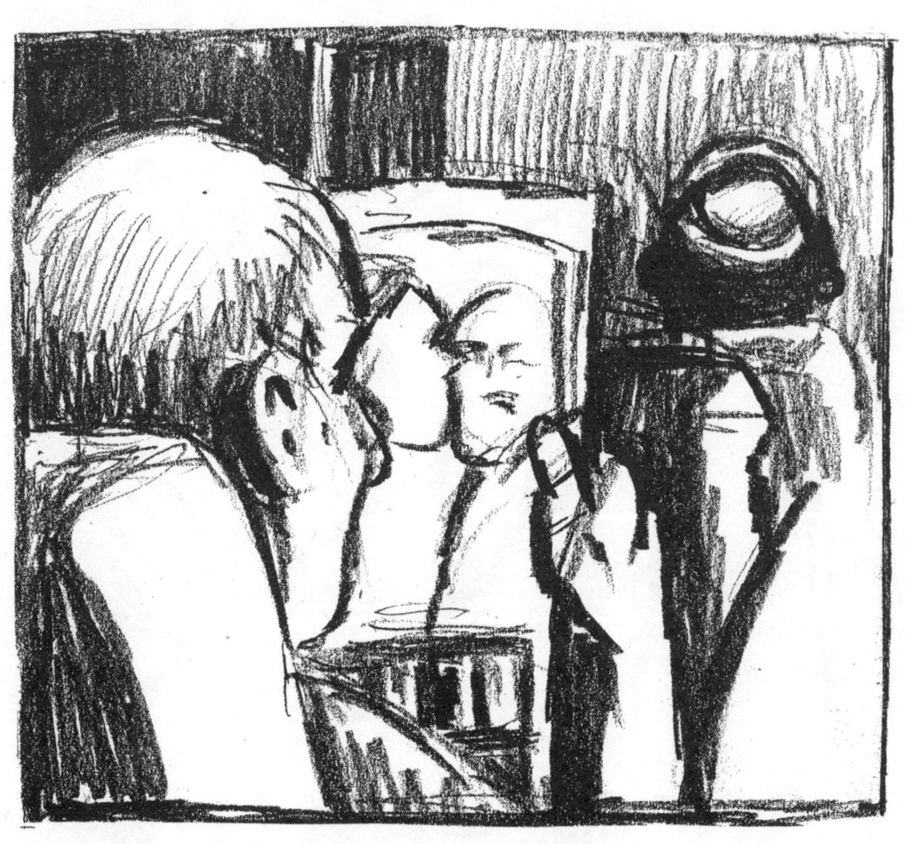

ON THE PLANE, THEY READ REPORTS OF THE LATEST BOMBING.

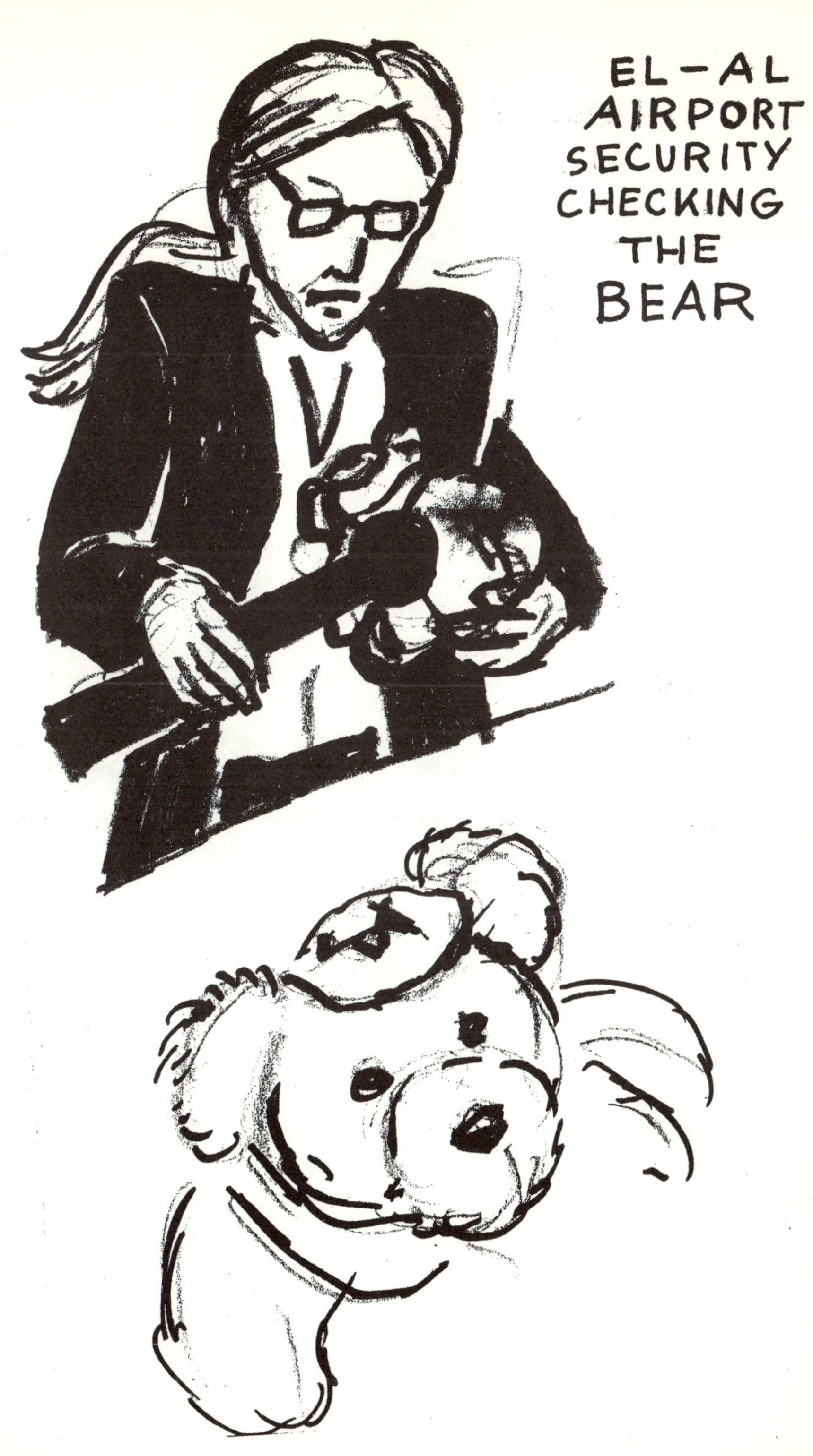
EL-AL
AIRPORT
SECURITY
CHECKING
THE
BEAR

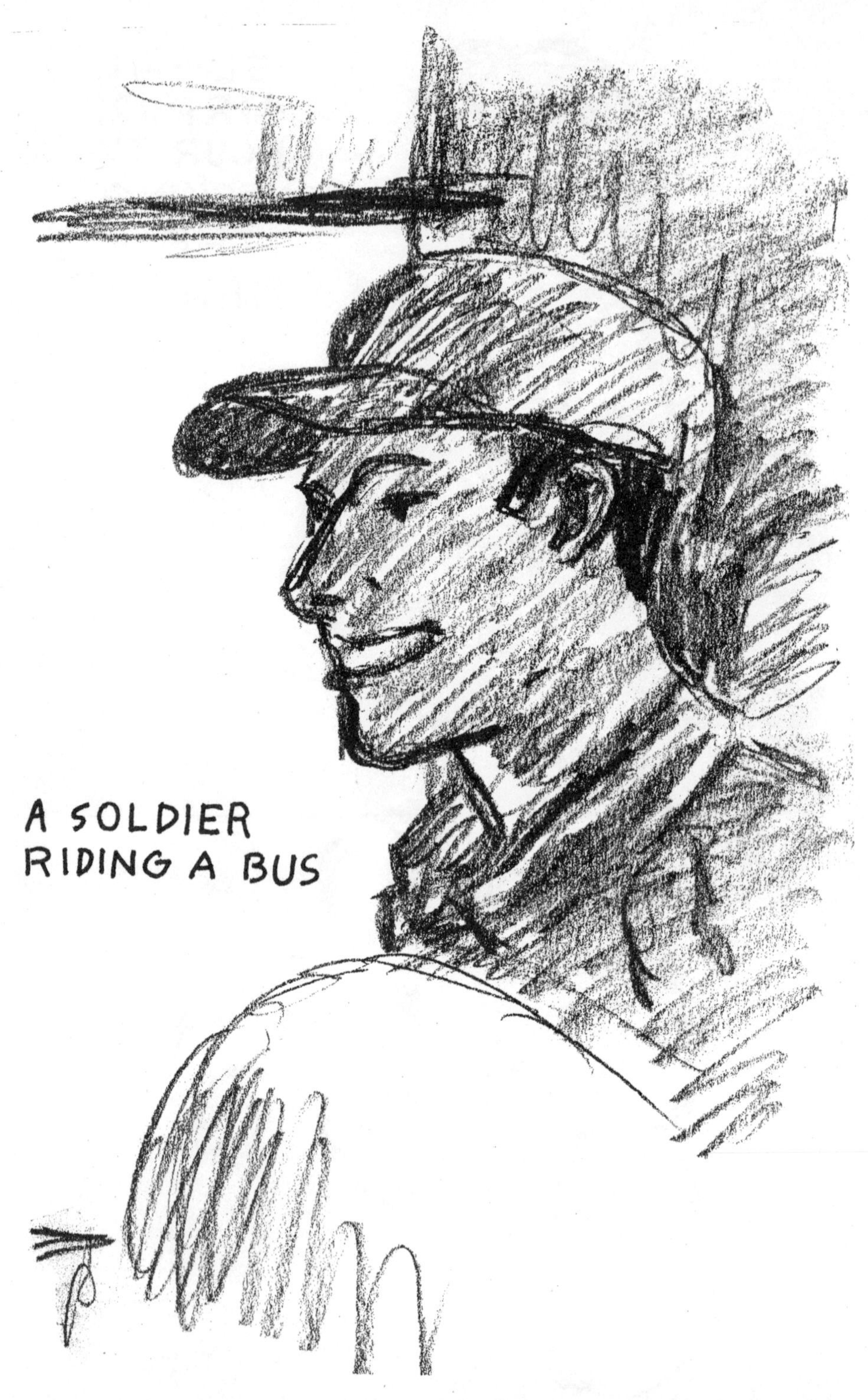
A SOLDIER
RIDING A BUS

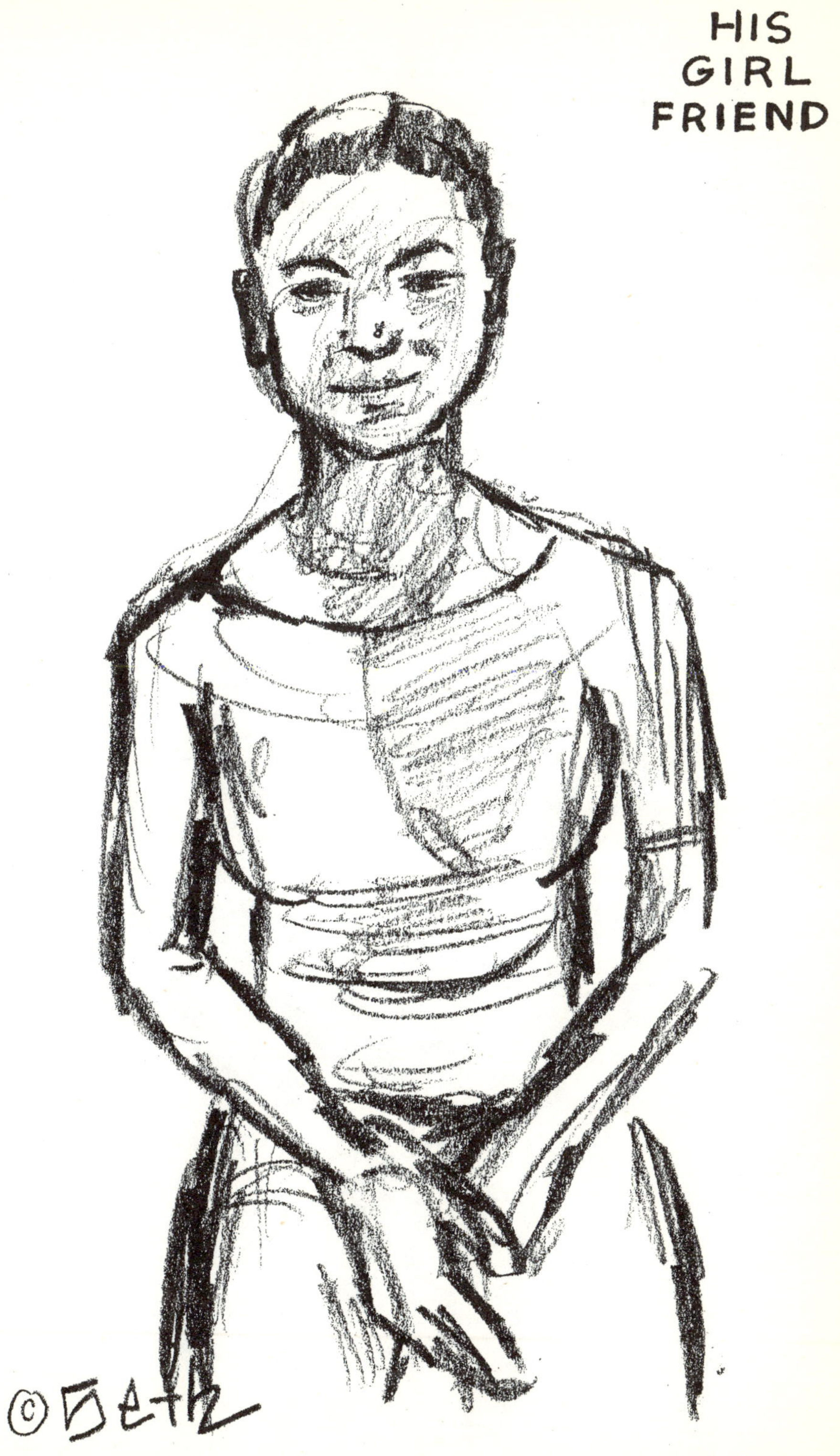
HIS
GIRL
FRIEND

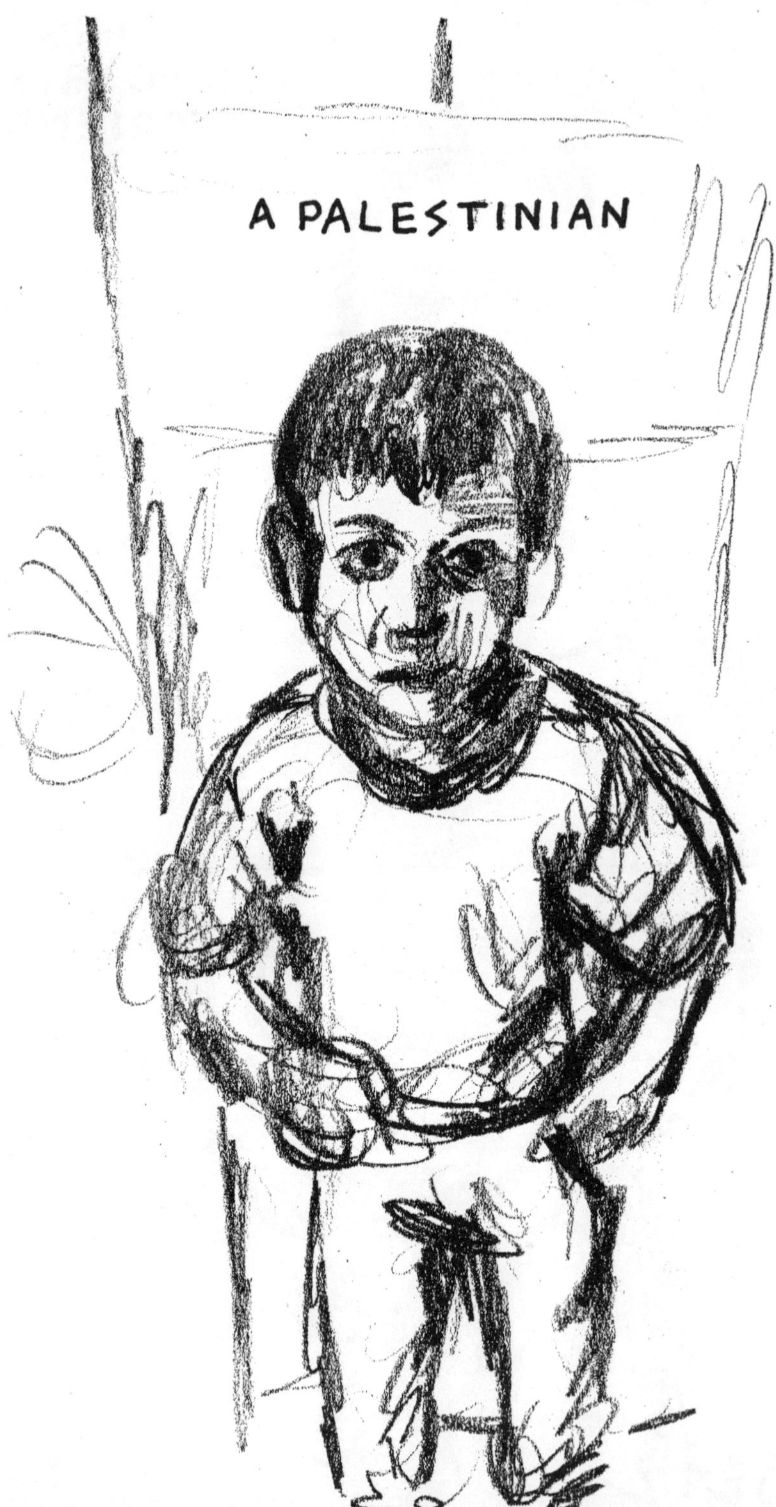
A PALESTINIAN

A PALESTINIAN CAB DRIVER,
HIS BROTHER LIVES IN
NEW YORK CITY.

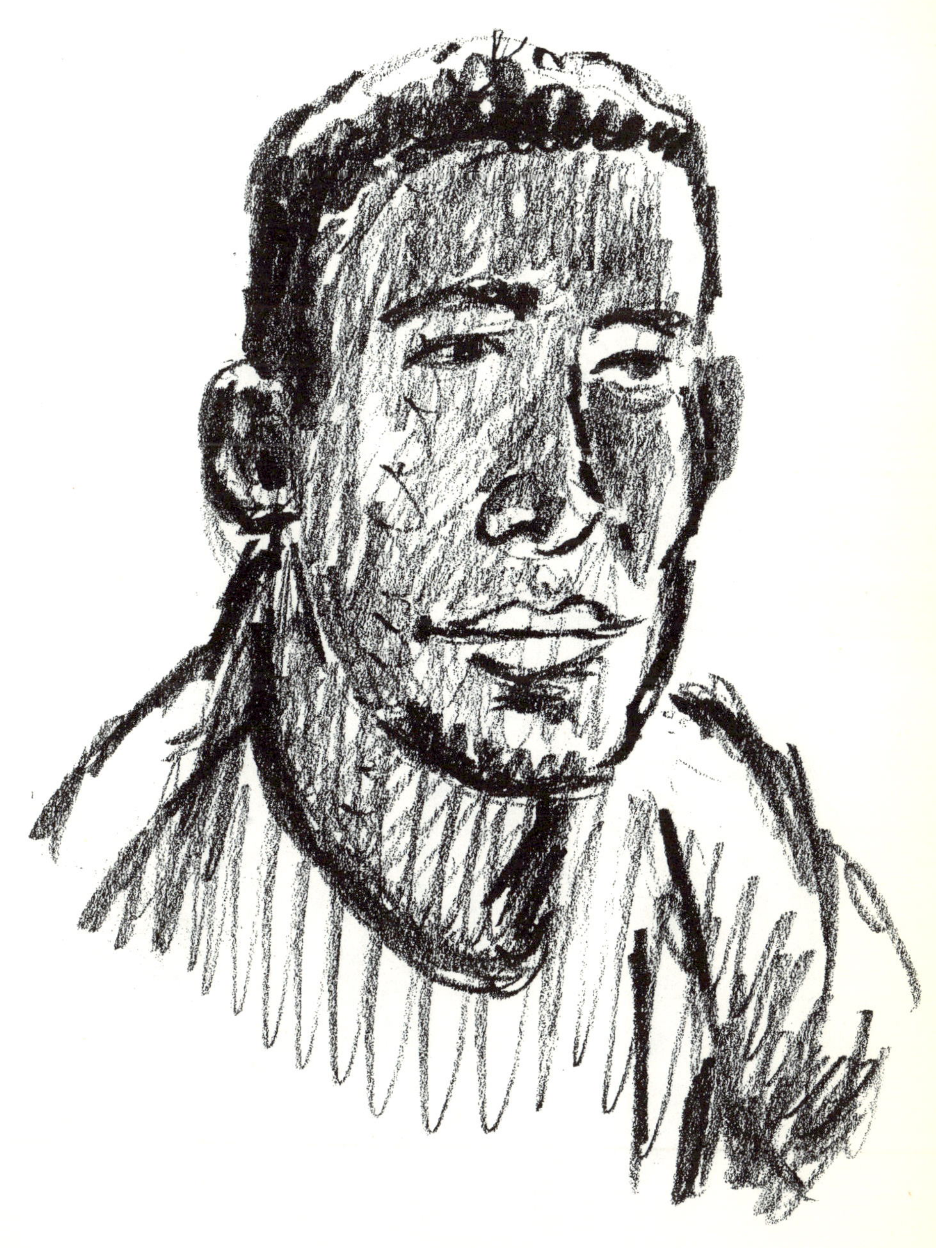

AND THESE TOO ARE PALESTINIANS.

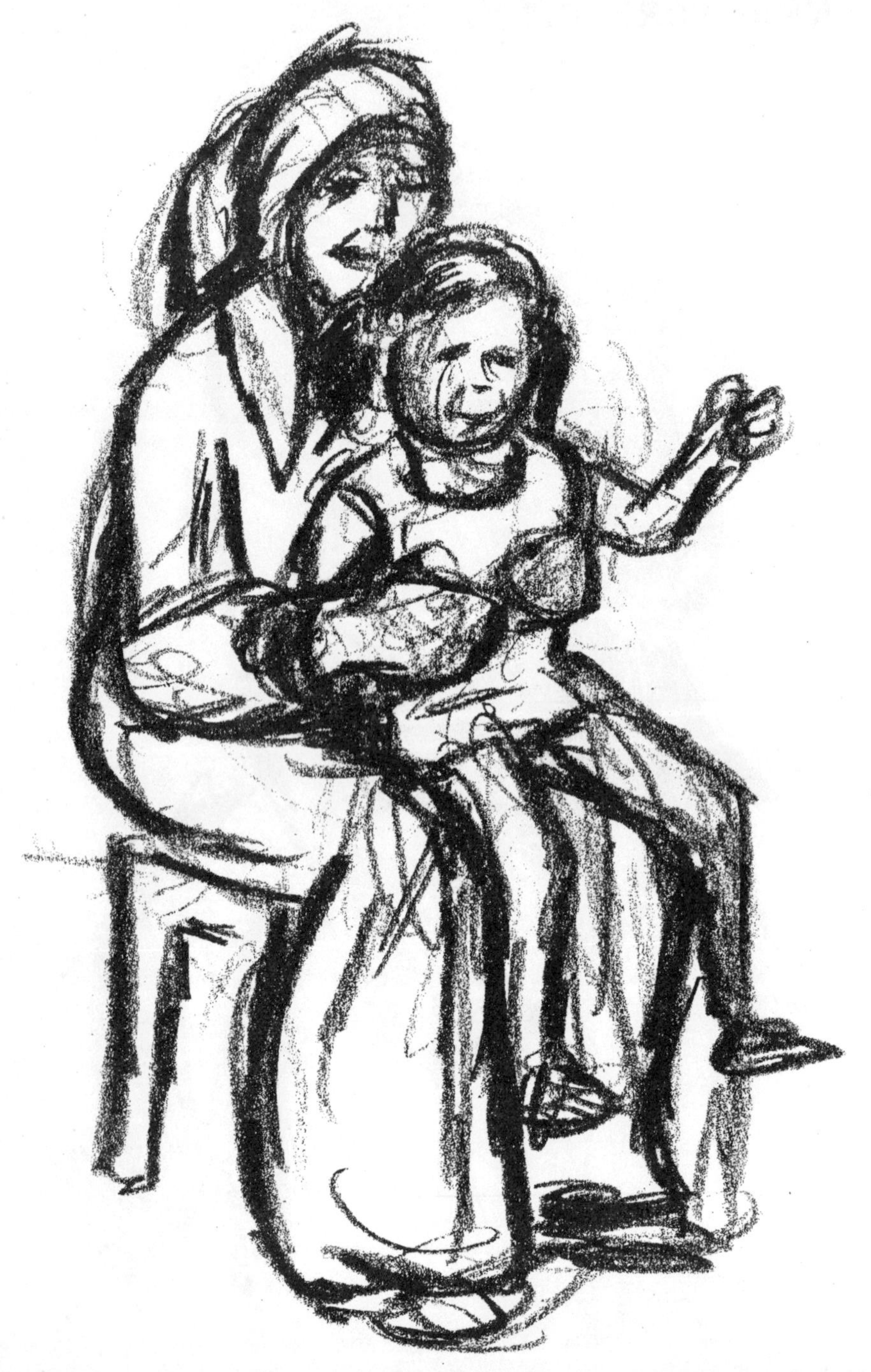

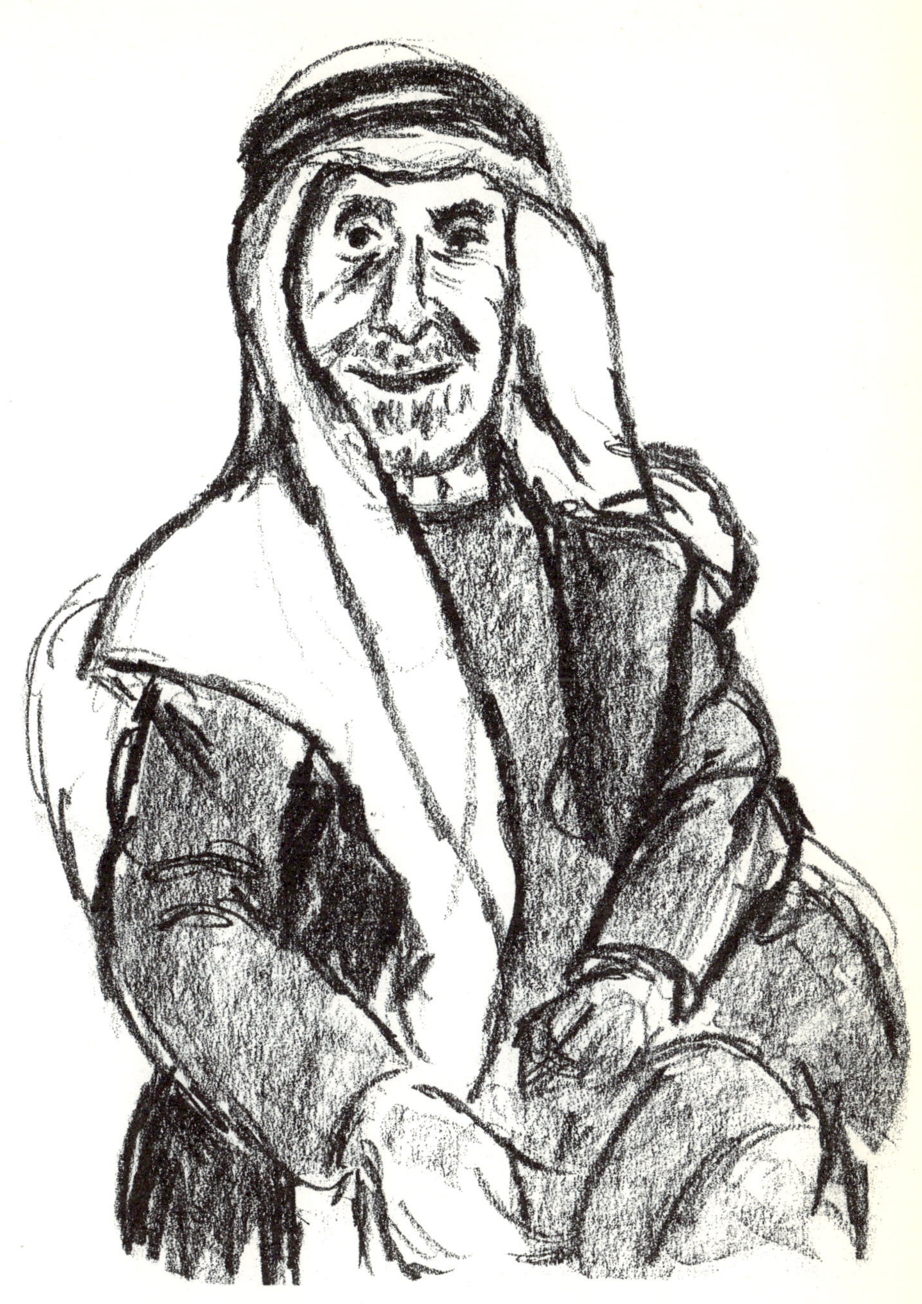

THIS FELLOW'S FRIENDS JOKE THAT HE USED TO WORK AS A TAX COLLECTOR FOR THE BRITISH.

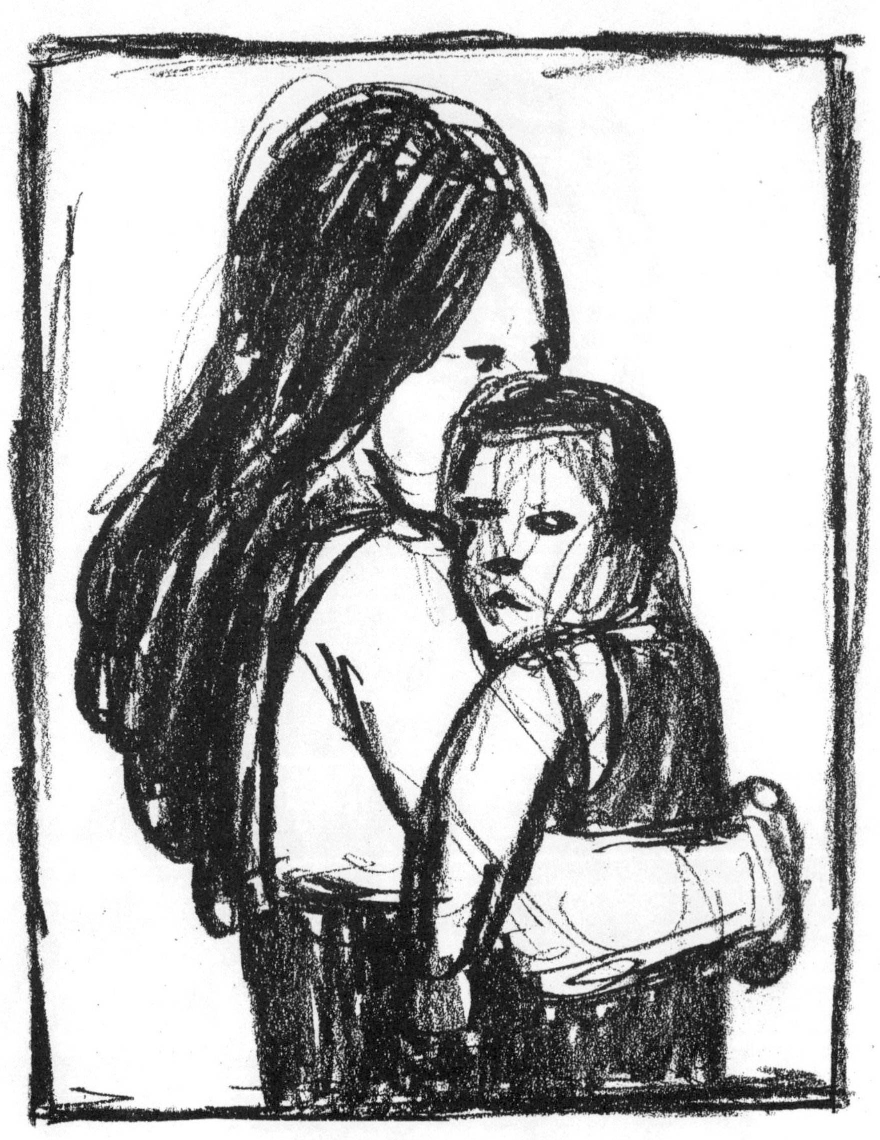

JEWS

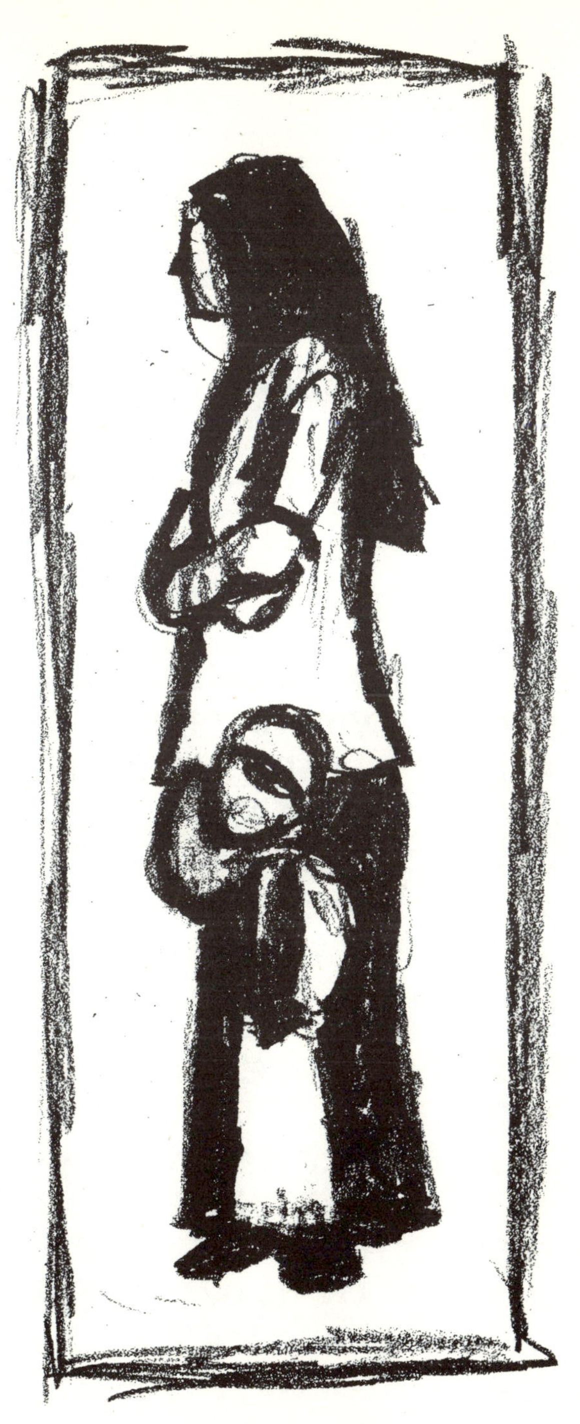

ARABS

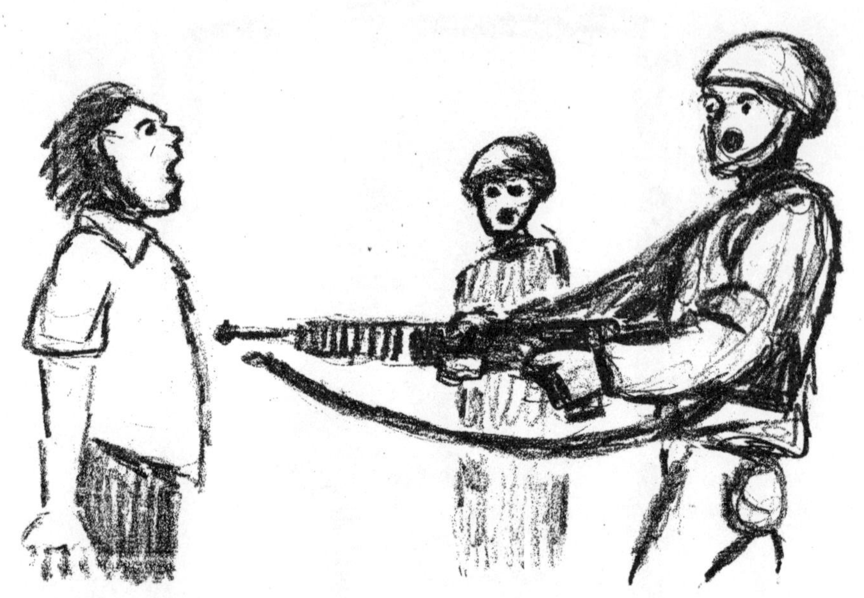

AND THIS IS HOW JEWS AND ARABS TEND TO INTERACT: A YOUNG MAN IS STOPPED BY TWO SOLDIERS WALKING THROUGH THE DAMASCUS GATE. MAYBE HE IS ON THE WAY TO WORK OR SCHOOL. THEY ARE HEAVILY ARMED BUT THEY SEEM TO BE SCARED. THEY THINK HE'S A TERRORIST. HE THINKS THEY ARE BASTARDS.

ISRAELIS AND PALESTINIANS ARE TWO COMMUNITIES AT WAR. BUT THEY ARE COMMUNITIES. COMMUNITIES WHERE PEOPLE LOVE THEIR CHILDREN, CARE FOR THEIR NEIGHBORS AND PARTICIPATE IN CIVIL SOCIETY. THEY ARE NOT CRAZY. THEY ARE NOT BARBARIANS. THEY ARE NOT EVIL.

ON MY 1ST DAY IN JERUSALEM, I SAT IN FRONT OF DAMASCUS GATE WITH MY SKETCH BOOK. ARAB KIDS CROWDED AROUND TO GET THEIR POR-TRAITS DRAWN. AS THE TINY BODIES PRESSED IN AROUND ME, I CAUGHT MYSELF LOOKING TO SEE IF THEY HAD BOMBS STRAPPED UNDER THEIR SHIRTS. THAT'S WHEN I REALIZED HOW MUCH I HAD BEEN BRAINWASHED BY THE MEDIA. FROM THAT MOMENT ON I WAS NOT AFRAID OF ANYONE I MET ON EITHER SIDE OF THE GREENLINE AND IN THIS I WAS NEVER WRONG.

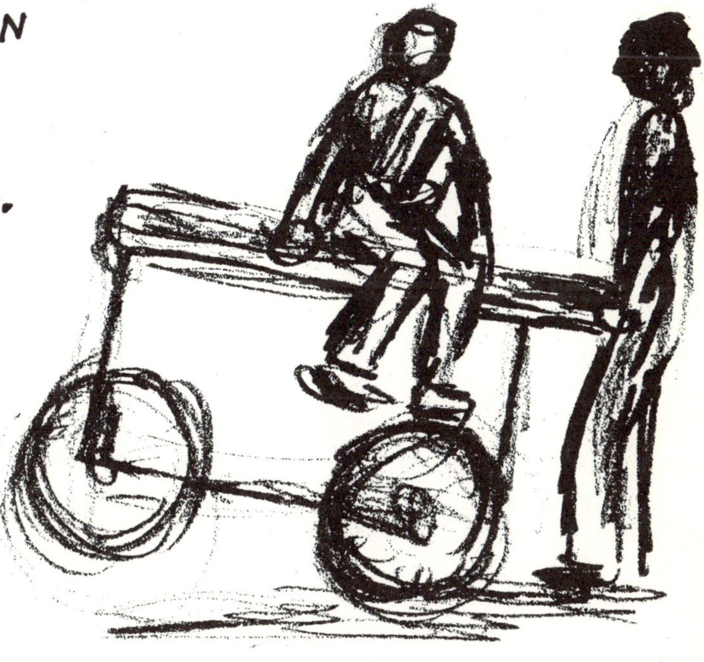

THE ORTHODOX

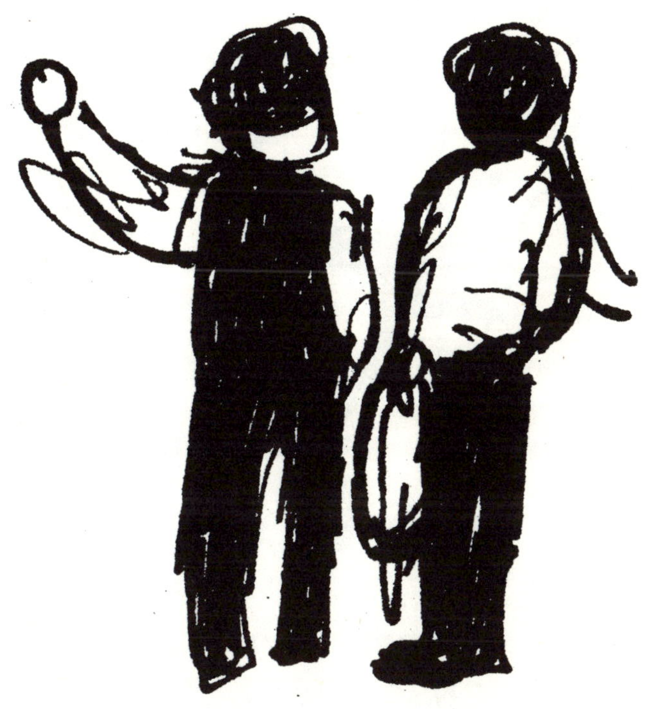

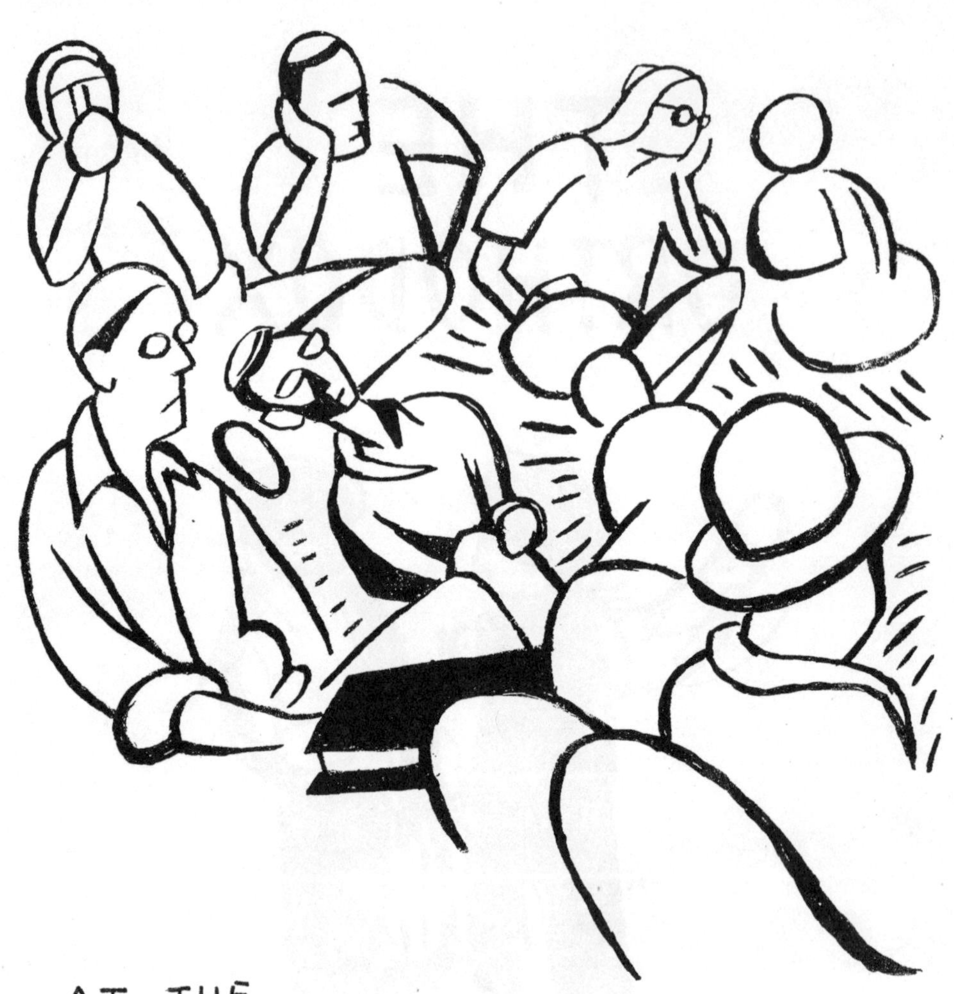

AT THE
RELIGIOUS
HOSTEL IN SAFED, THE RABBI EXPLAINS THAT FOR GENERATIONS, THE STUDY OF KABALAH (JEWISH MYSTICISM), WAS RESTRICTED TO THOSE LEARNED ENOUGH TO APPRECIATE ITS MEANING. BUT TODAY, WHEN MANY ARE LEAVING THE FAITH, IT HAS BEEN FOUND THAT KABALAH ATTRACTS YOUNG JEWS TO TRADITION.

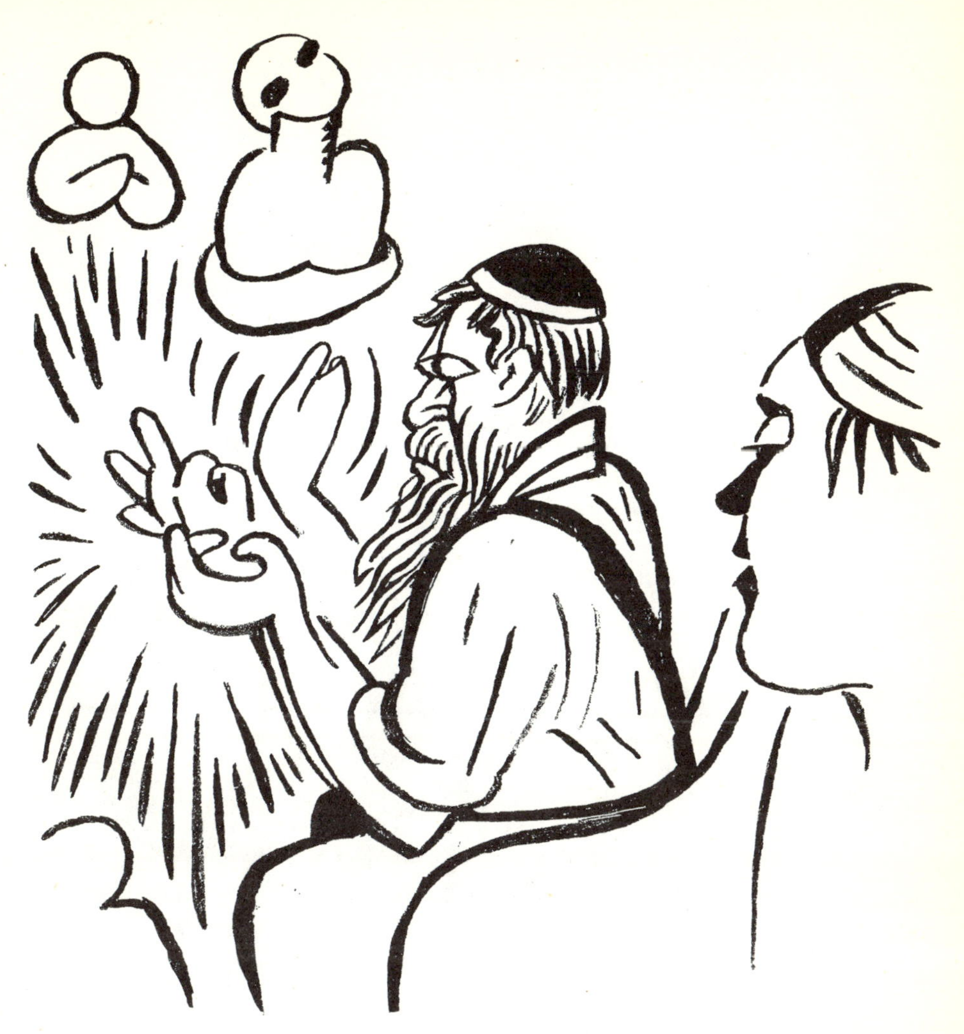

AND SO LESSONS IN THE KABALAH ARE NOW MADE AVAILABLE TO THE MASSES.

2 YOUNG MEN

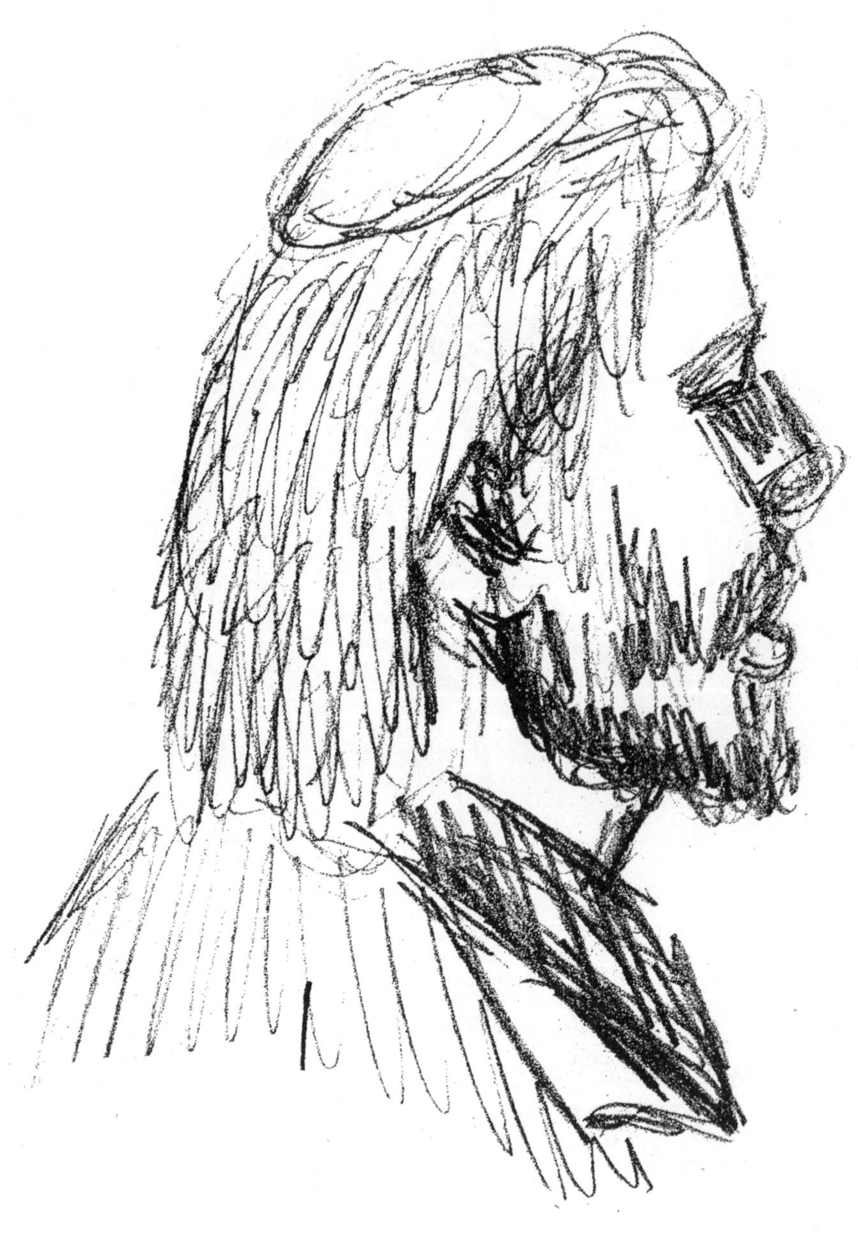

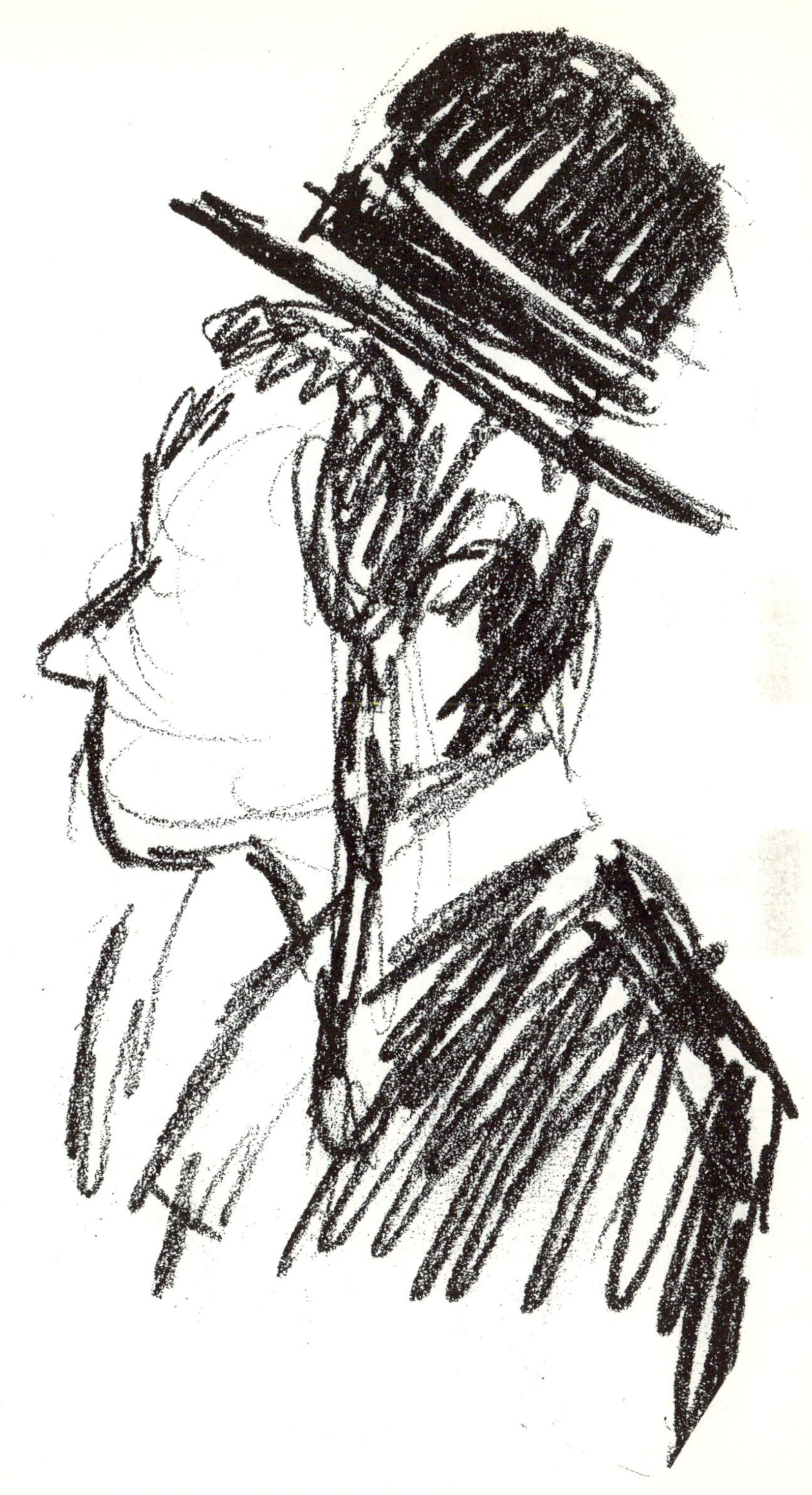

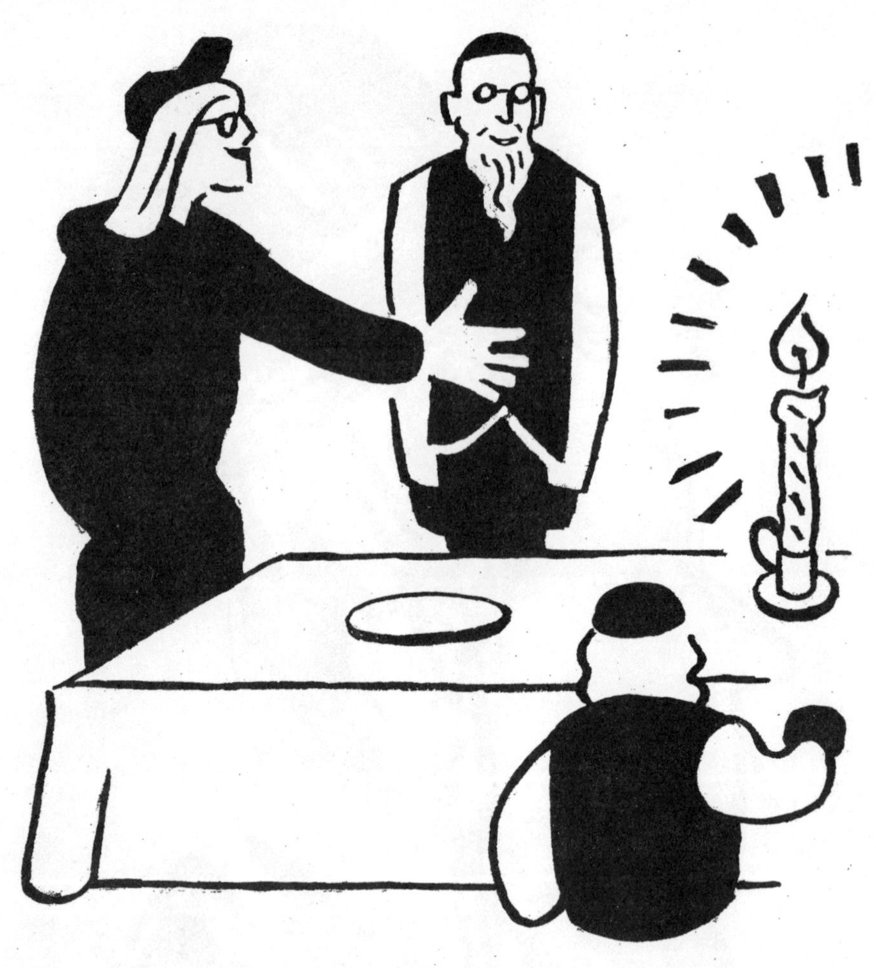

MANY OF THE WOMEN IN SAFED POLITELY REFUSE TO SHAKE HANDS WITH GUYS. THEY DO NOT TOUCH MEN OTHER THAN THEIR HUSBANDS. THEY KEEP HAIR, SHOULDERS AND LEGS COVERED.

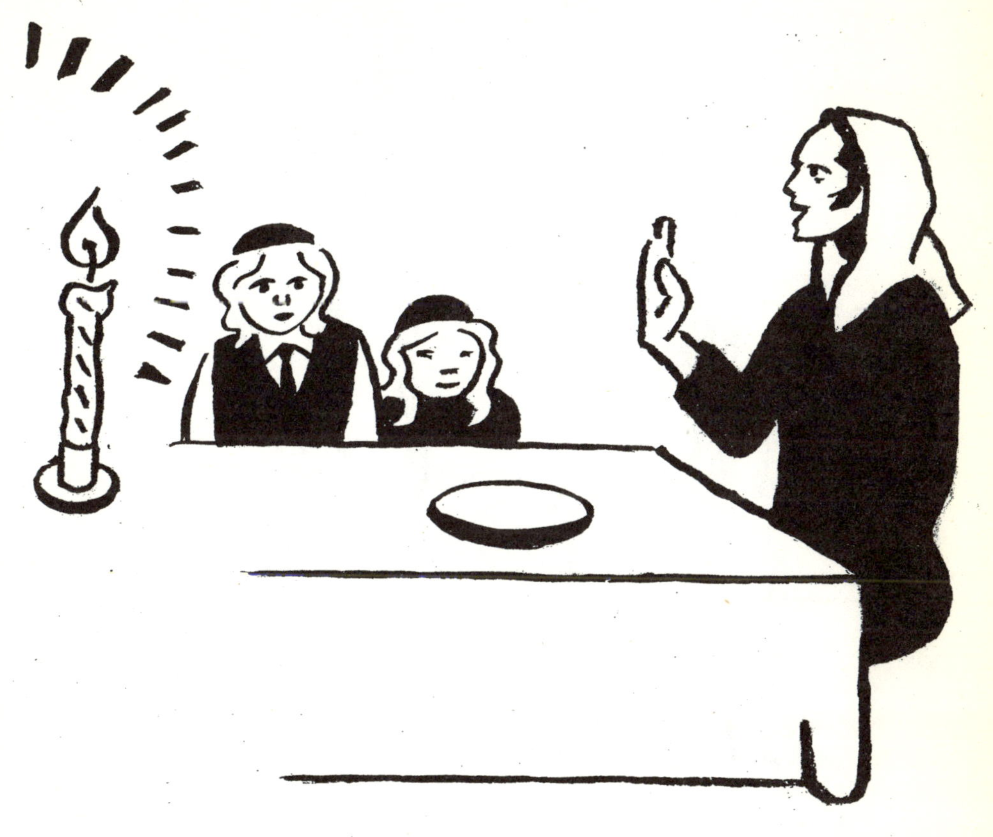

IN **SAFED** I MET MANY AMERICAN AND EUROPEAN WOMEN WHO INSISTED THAT THESE MEDIEVAL CUSTOMS WERE VERY LIBERATING.

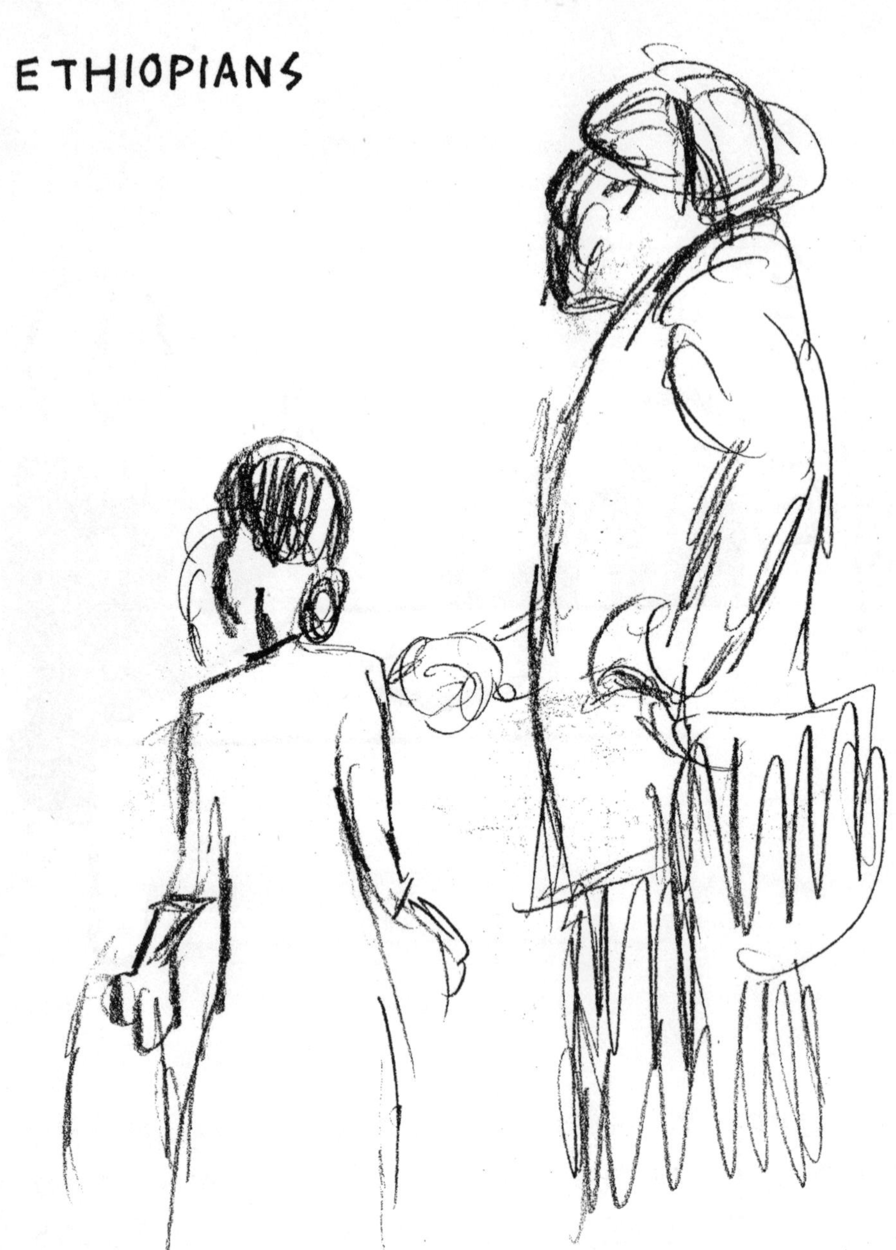
ETHIOPIANS

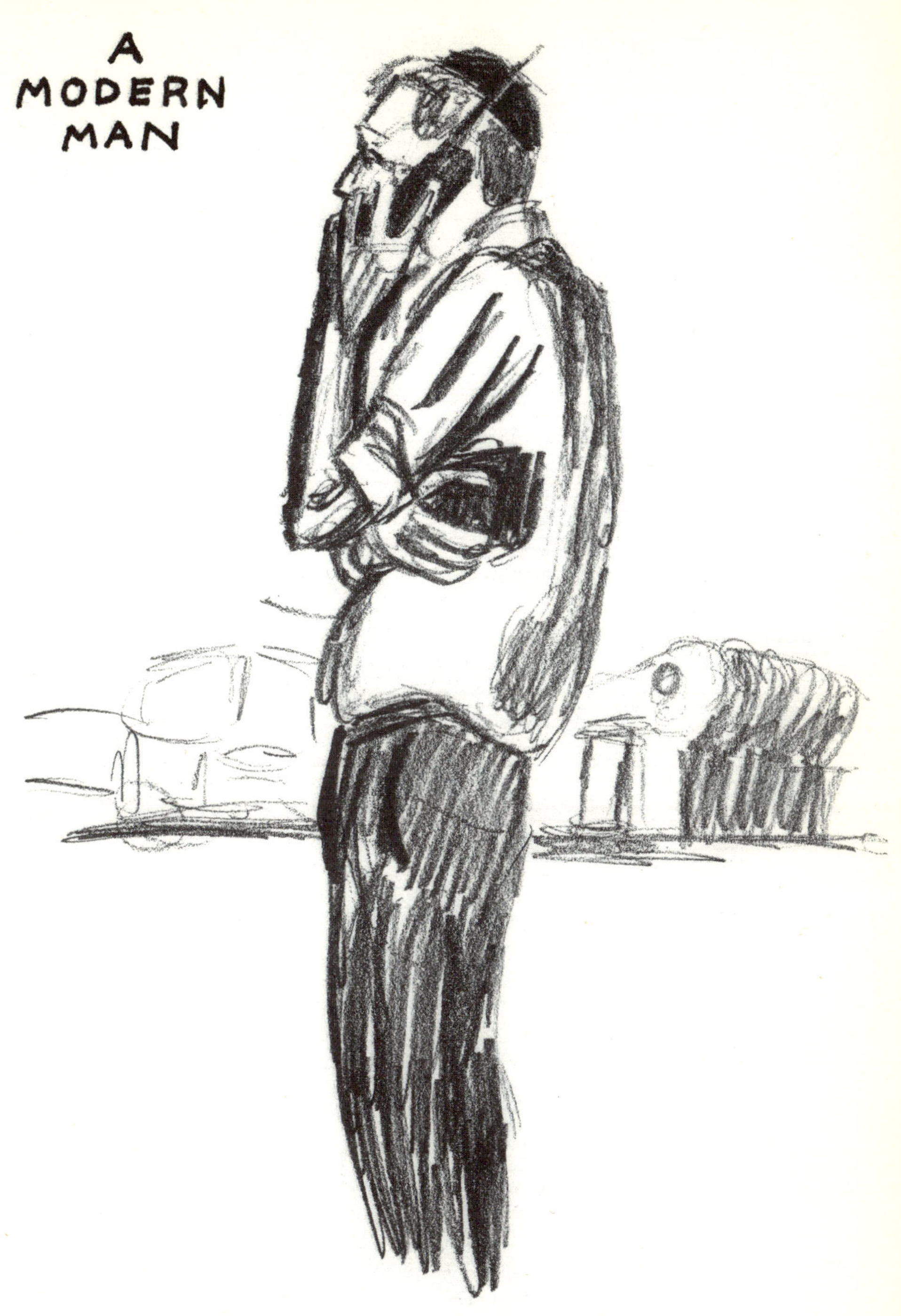
A
MODERN
MAN

THIS CALIFORNIAN SPENDS 5 MONTHS A YEAR TEACHING RELIGION IN SAFED. HE SAYS HE SERVED AS A CIVILIAN VOLUNTEER IN THE 6 DAY WAR, BUT HE COULD NOT JOIN THE ISRAELI ARMY BE-CAUSE HE'D LOSE HIS U.S. CITIZENSHIP.

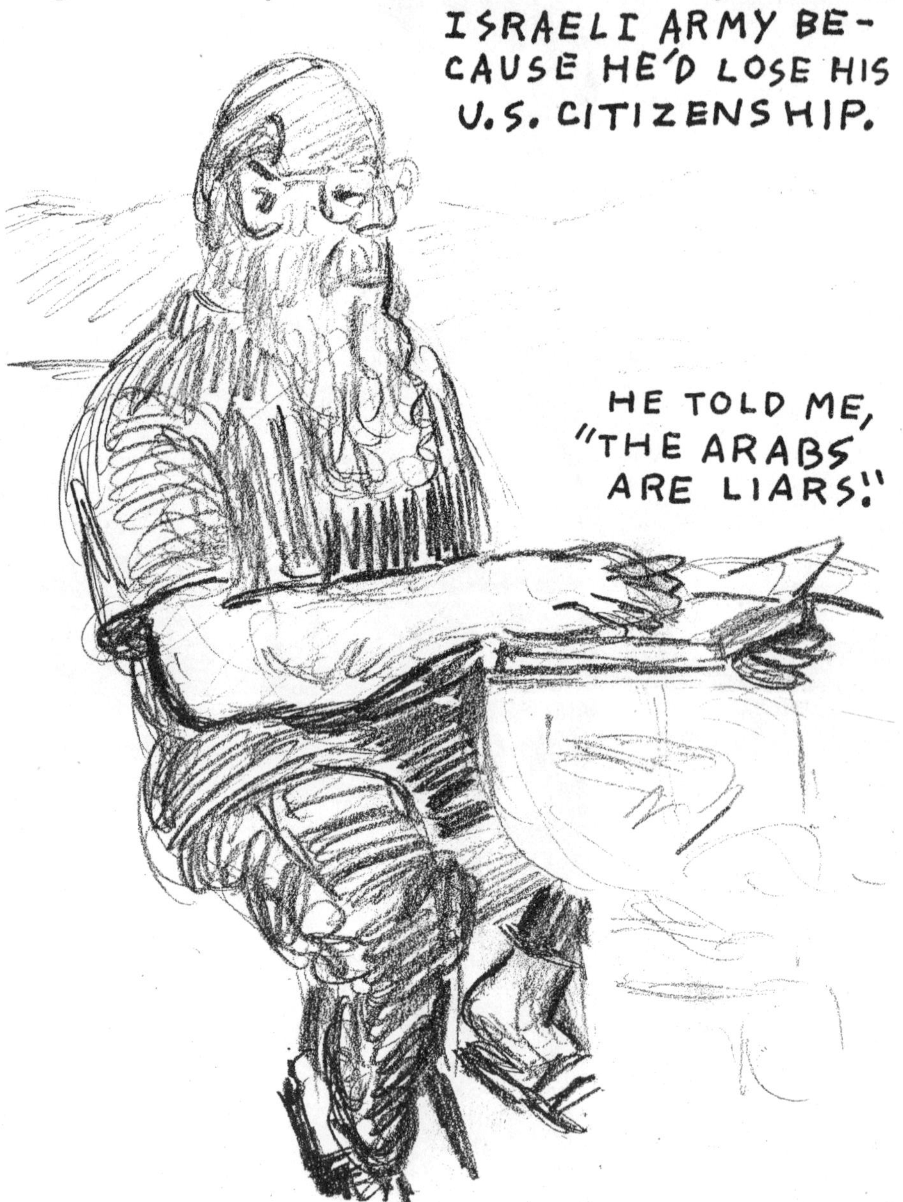

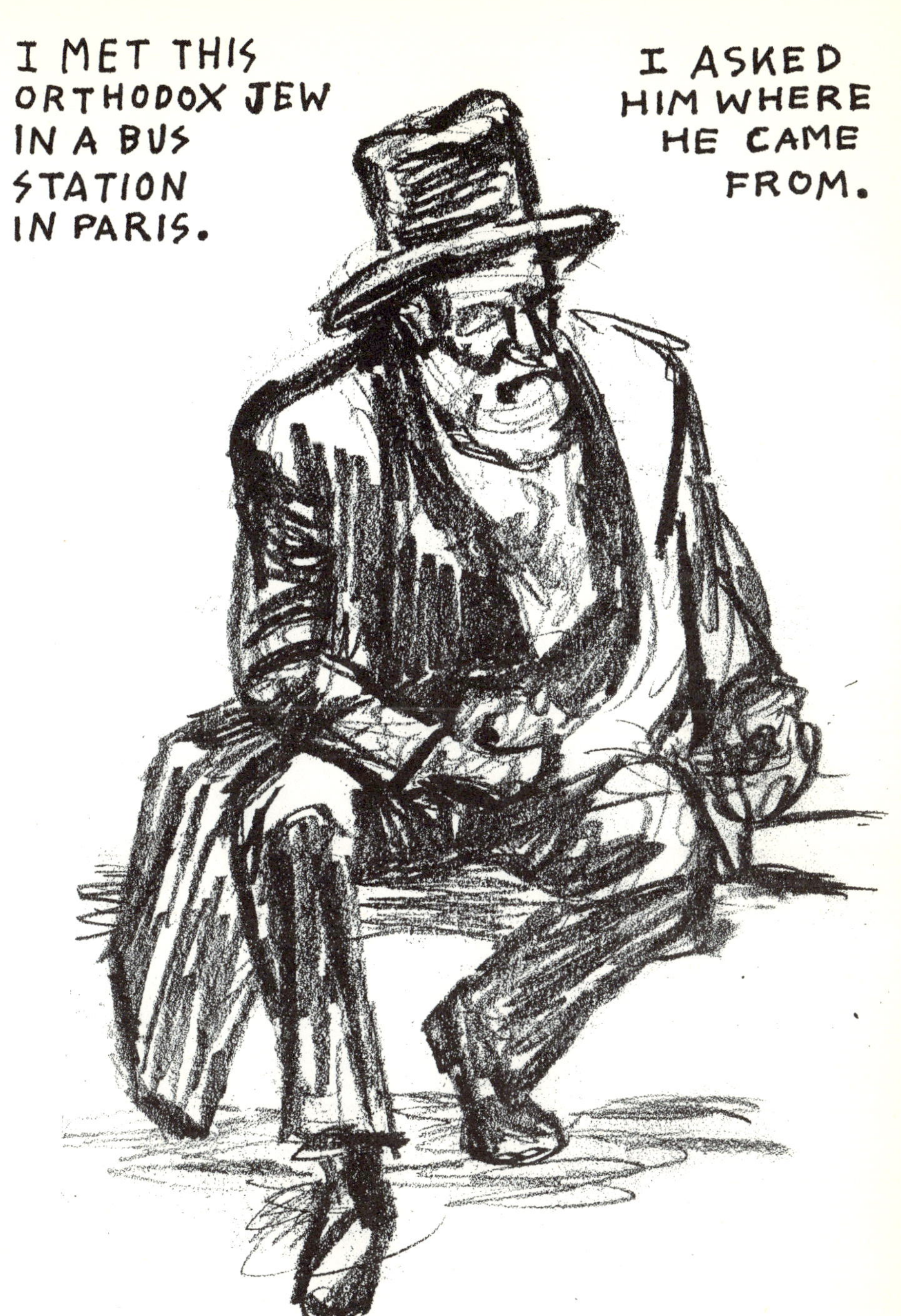
I MET THIS ORTHODOX JEW IN A BUS STATION IN PARIS.
I ASKED HIM WHERE HE CAME FROM.
HE SAID HE CAME FROM PALESTINE.

The Beautiful Village

THE PALESTINIAN VILLAGE OF DIRIBZIA IS LOCATED IN THE HILLS NEAR RAMALLAH. THE NAME MEANS "VILLAGE WITH A CHURCH"

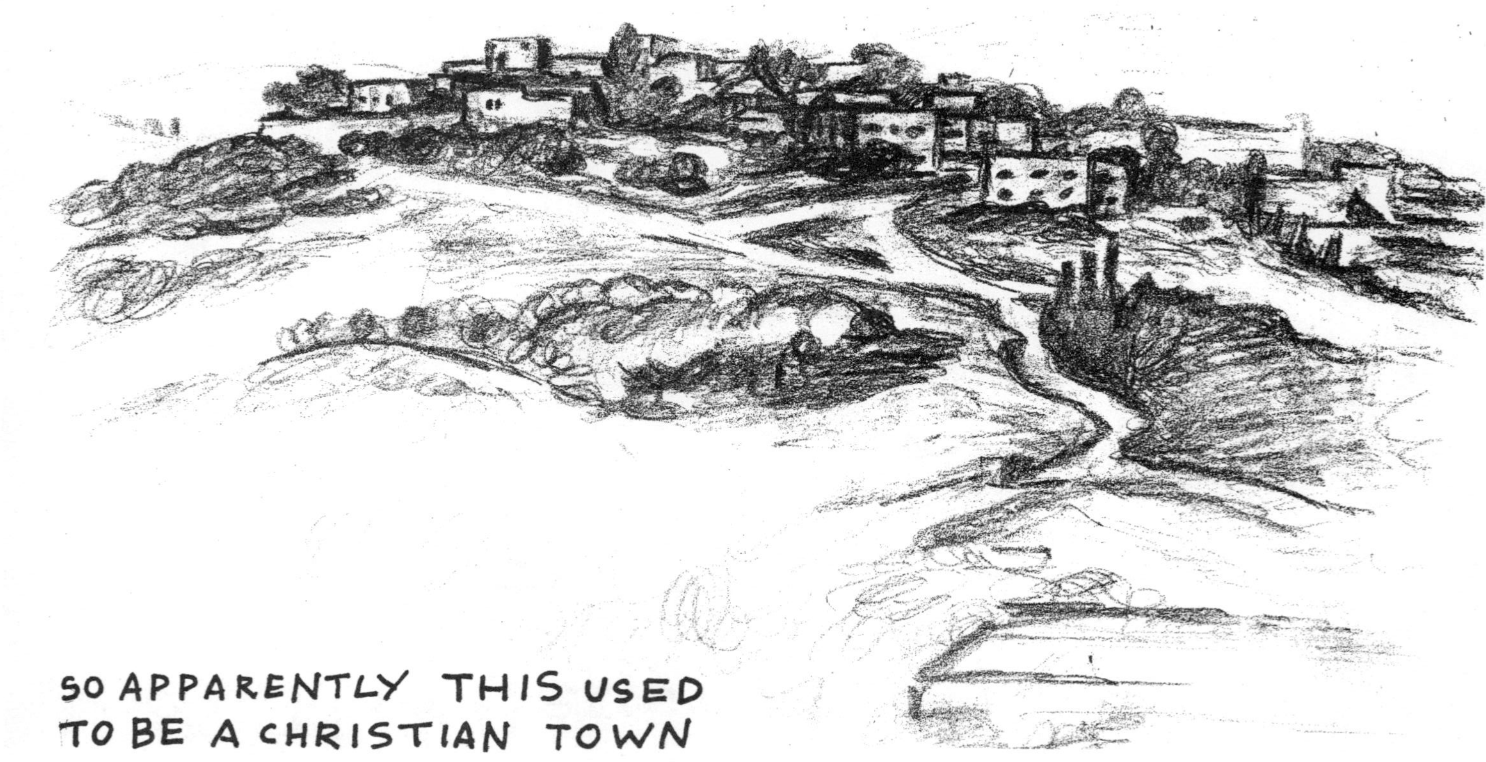

SO APPARENTLY THIS USED TO BE A CHRISTIAN TOWN

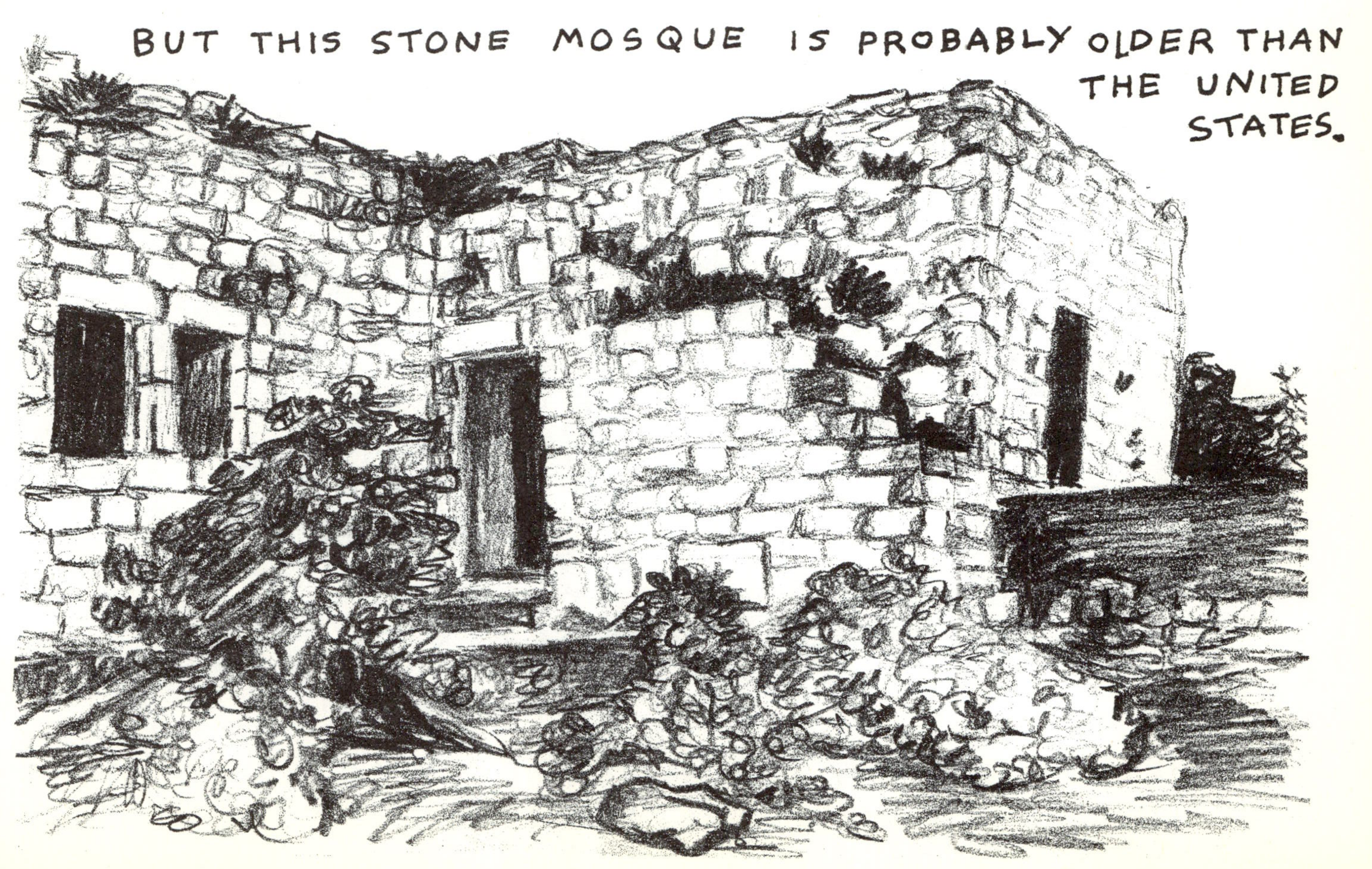
BUT THIS STONE MOSQUE IS PROBABLY OLDER THAN THE UNITED STATES.

BUT THERE ARE ALSO NEW STRUCTURES. BUILT BY MIDDLE CLASS PALESTINIANS FROM THE U.S. AND EUROPE, WHO RETURNED AFTER OSLO.

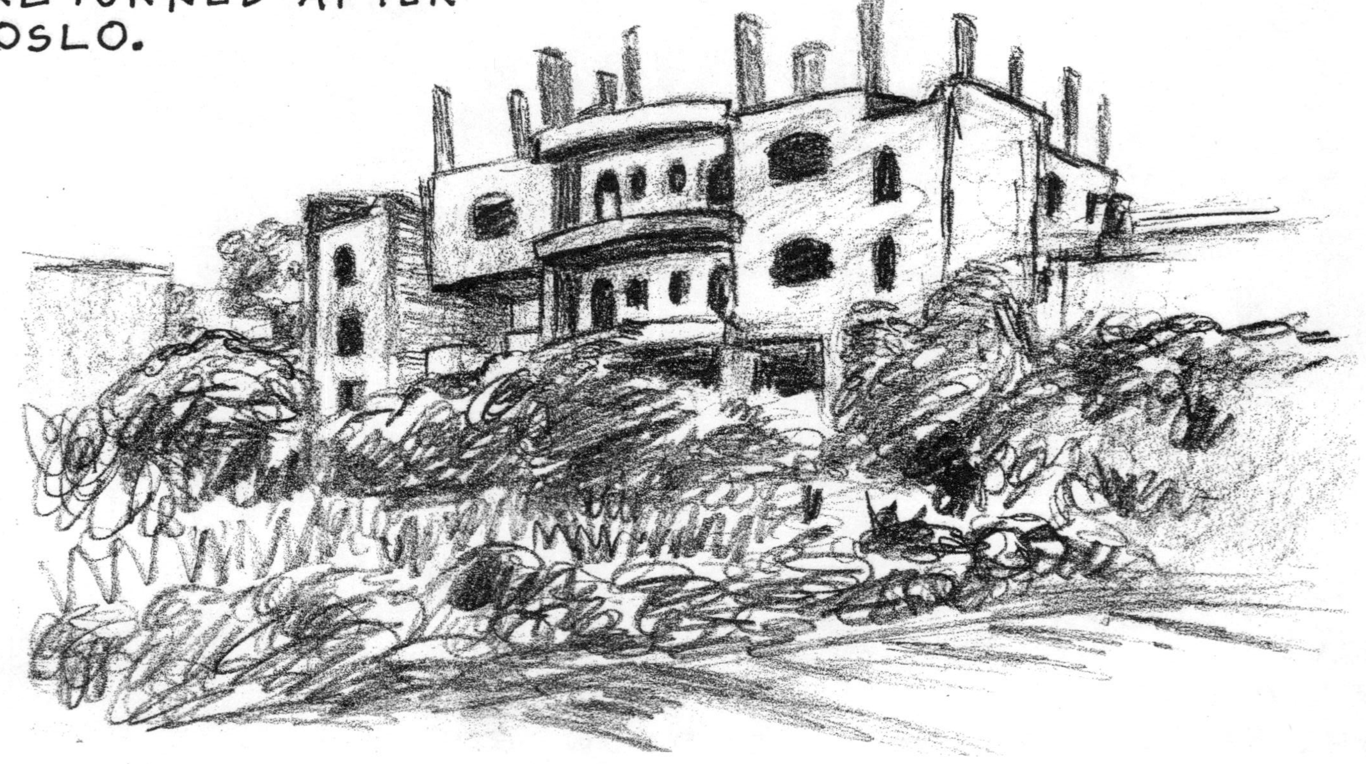

NOW, BECAUSE OF THE WAR, THEY HAVE LEFT THEIR HOUSES UNFINISHED.

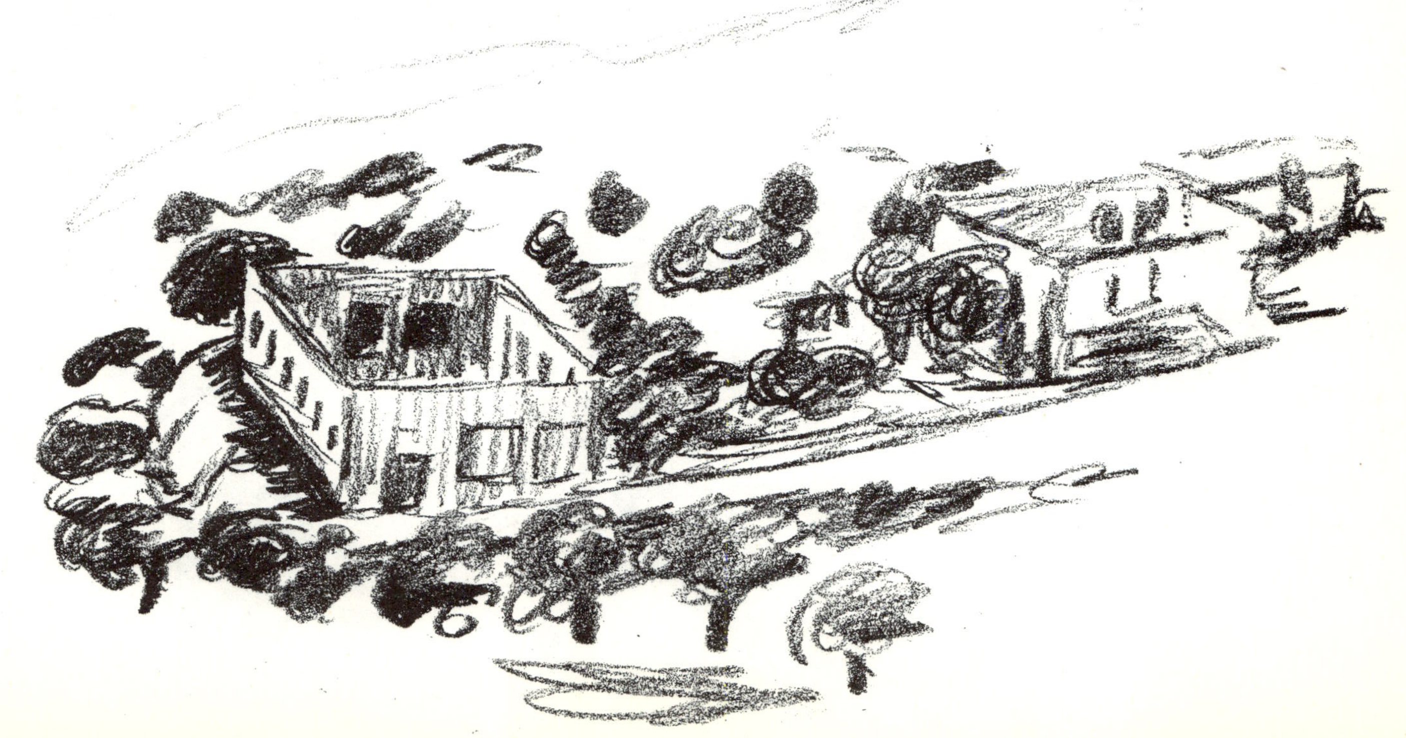

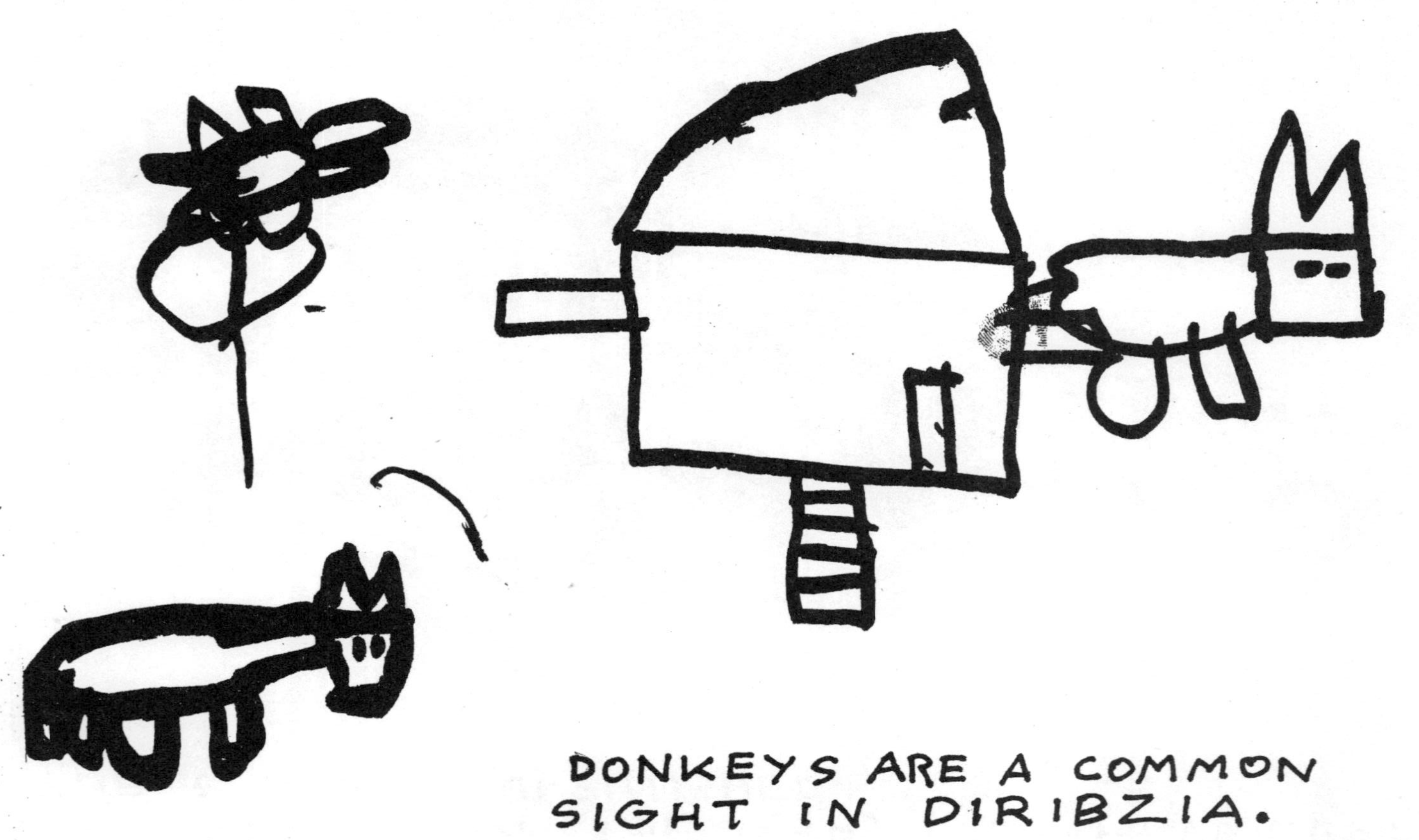

DONKEYS ARE A COMMON SIGHT IN DIRIBZIA.

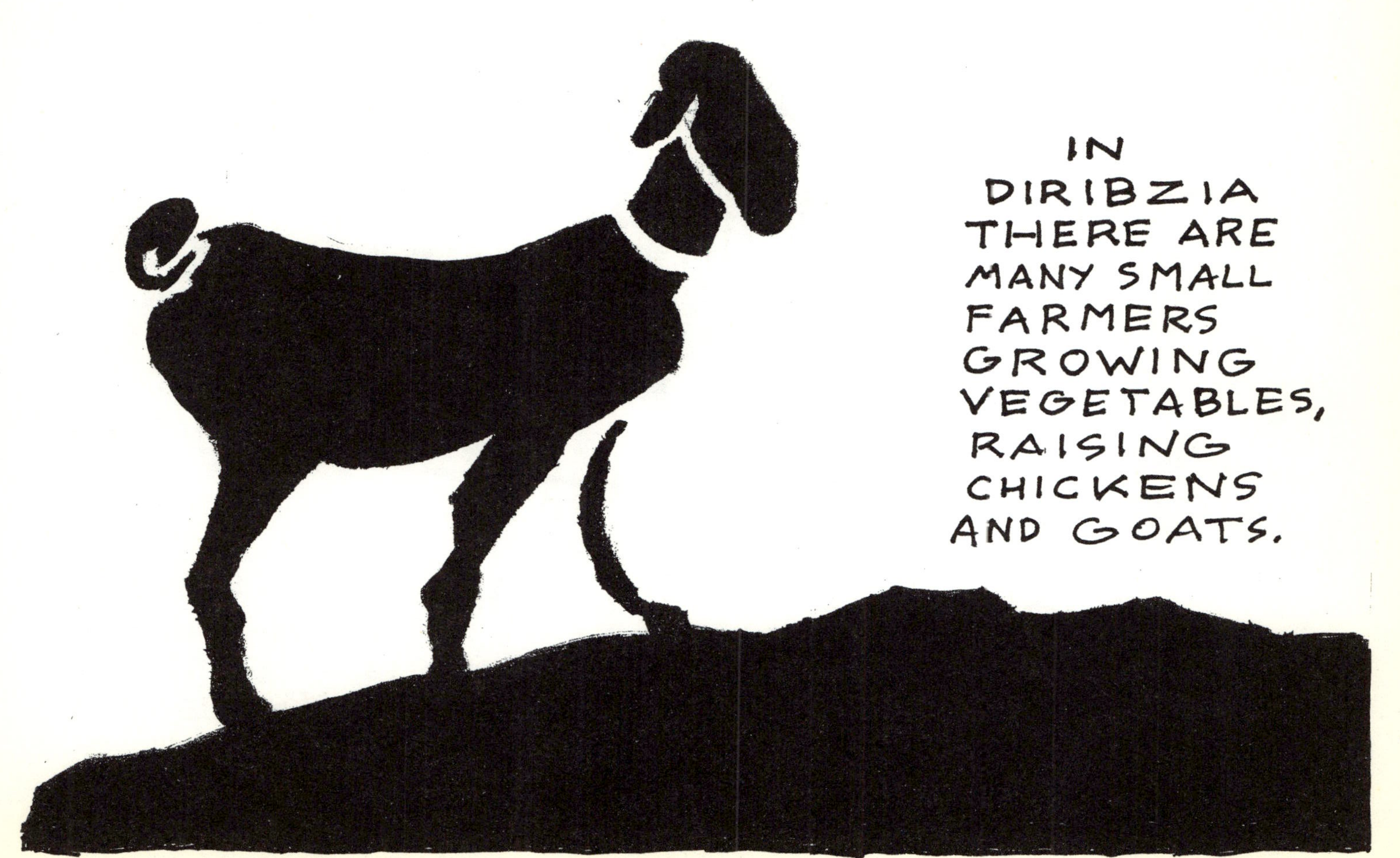
IN
DIRIBZIA
THERE ARE
MANY SMALL
FARMERS
GROWING
VEGETABLES,
RAISING
CHICKENS
AND GOATS.

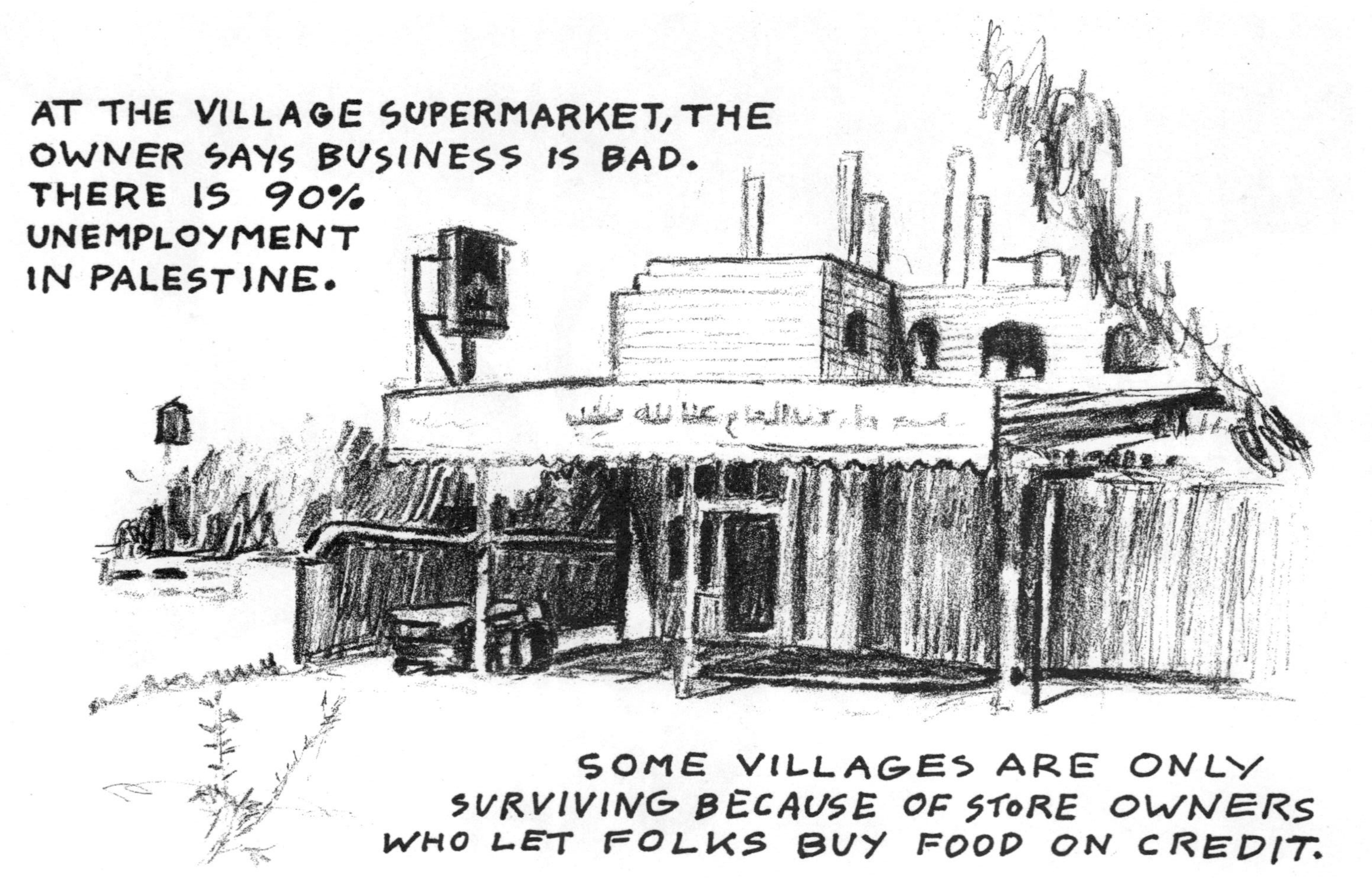
AT THE VILLAGE SUPERMARKET, THE OWNER SAYS BUSINESS IS BAD. THERE IS 90% UNEMPLOYMENT IN PALESTINE.
SOME VILLAGES ARE ONLY SURVIVING BECAUSE OF STORE OWNERS WHO LET FOLKS BUY FOOD ON CREDIT.

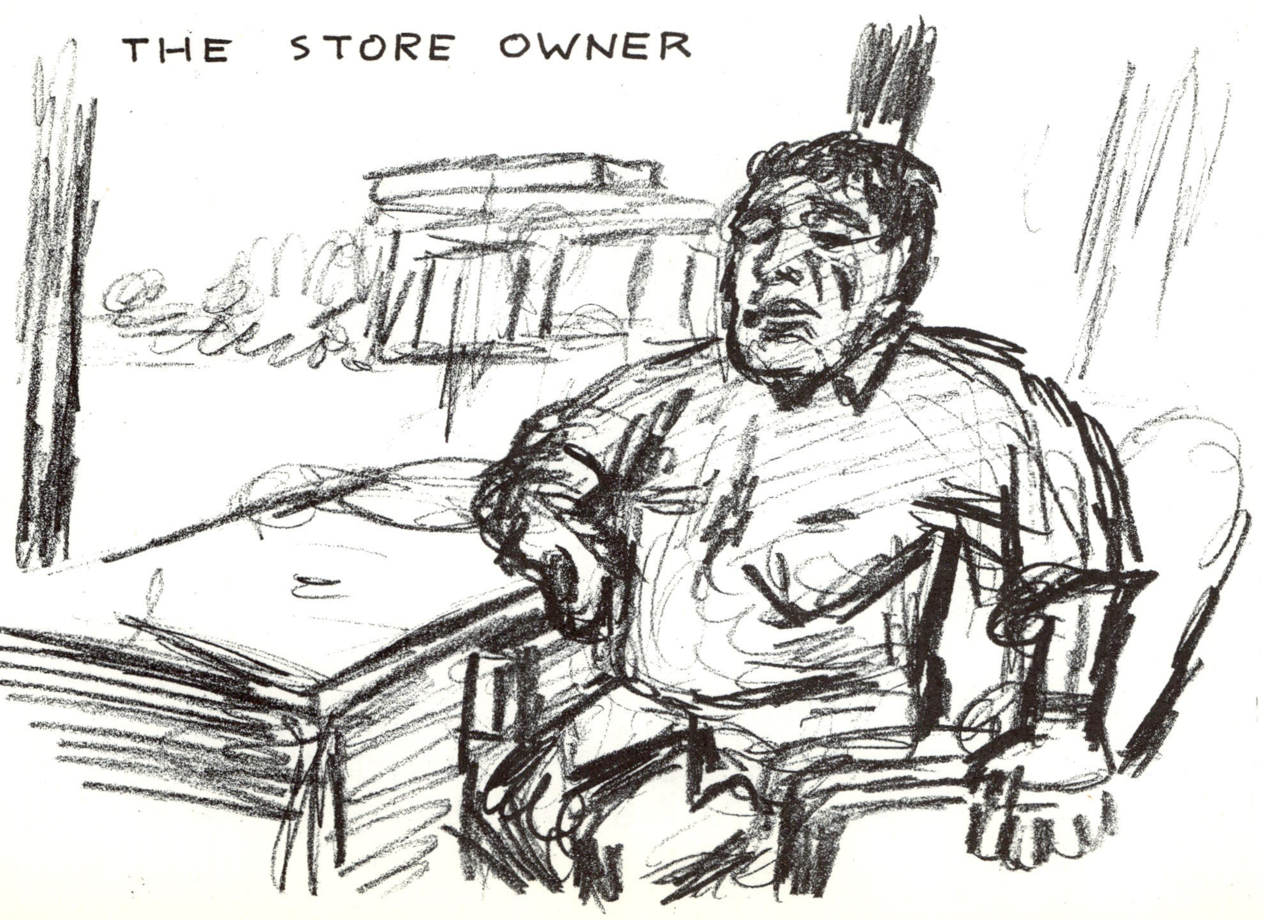
THE STORE OWNER
HAS
ONE
BAD
LEG.
IN
HIS
STORE
THERE
ARE
MANY
CHIL-
DREN
AND
FEW
CUS-
TOM
-ERS.

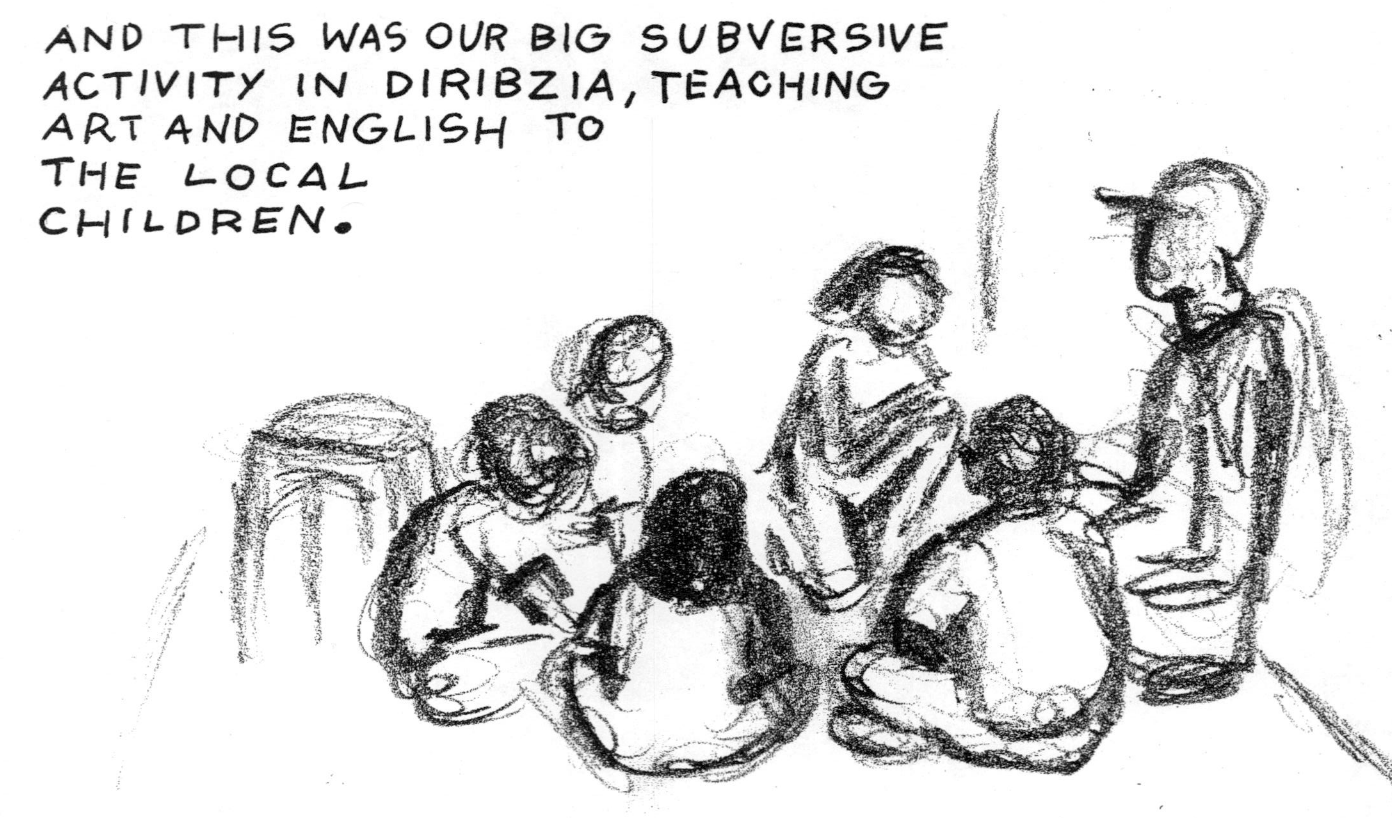
AND THIS WAS OUR BIG SUBVERSIVE
ACTIVITY IN DIRIBZIA, TEACHING
ART AND ENGLISH TO
THE LOCAL
CHILDREN.

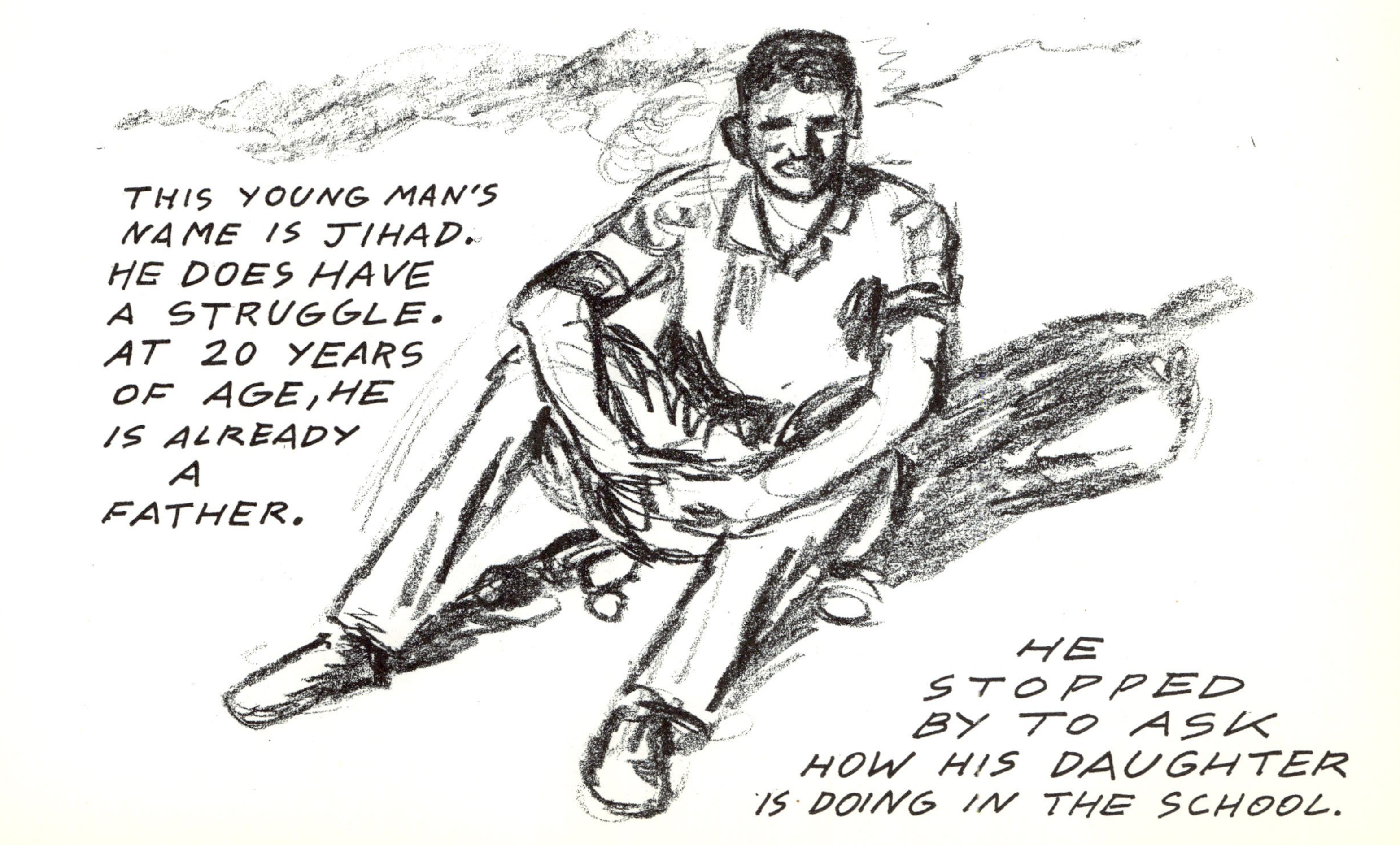
THIS YOUNG MAN'S
NAME IS JIHAD.
HE DOES HAVE
A STRUGGLE.
AT 20 YEARS
OF AGE, HE
IS ALREADY
A
FATHER.
HE
STOPPED
BY TO ASK
HOW HIS DAUGHTER
IS DOING IN THE SCHOOL.

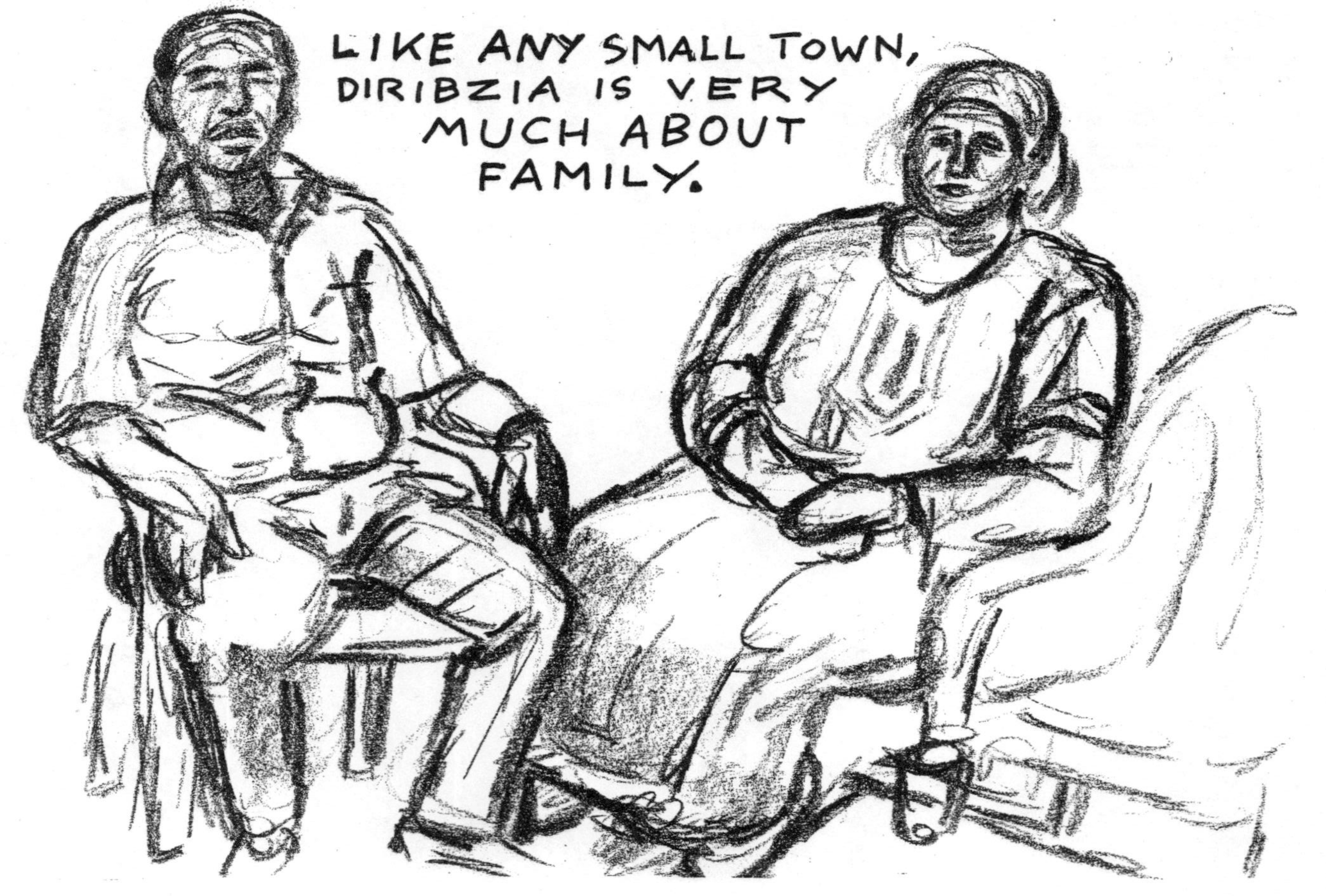
LIKE ANY SMALL TOWN,
DIRIBZIA IS VERY
MUCH ABOUT
FAMILY.

THE ONLY PLACE WHERE DIRIBZIA CHILDREN CAN SWIM ON HOT DAYS IS A CONCRETE IRRIGATION TANK FULL OF FOUL SMELLING GREENISH BROWN WATER. THE BOYS NONE THE LESS JUMP IN ENTHUSIASTICALLY.

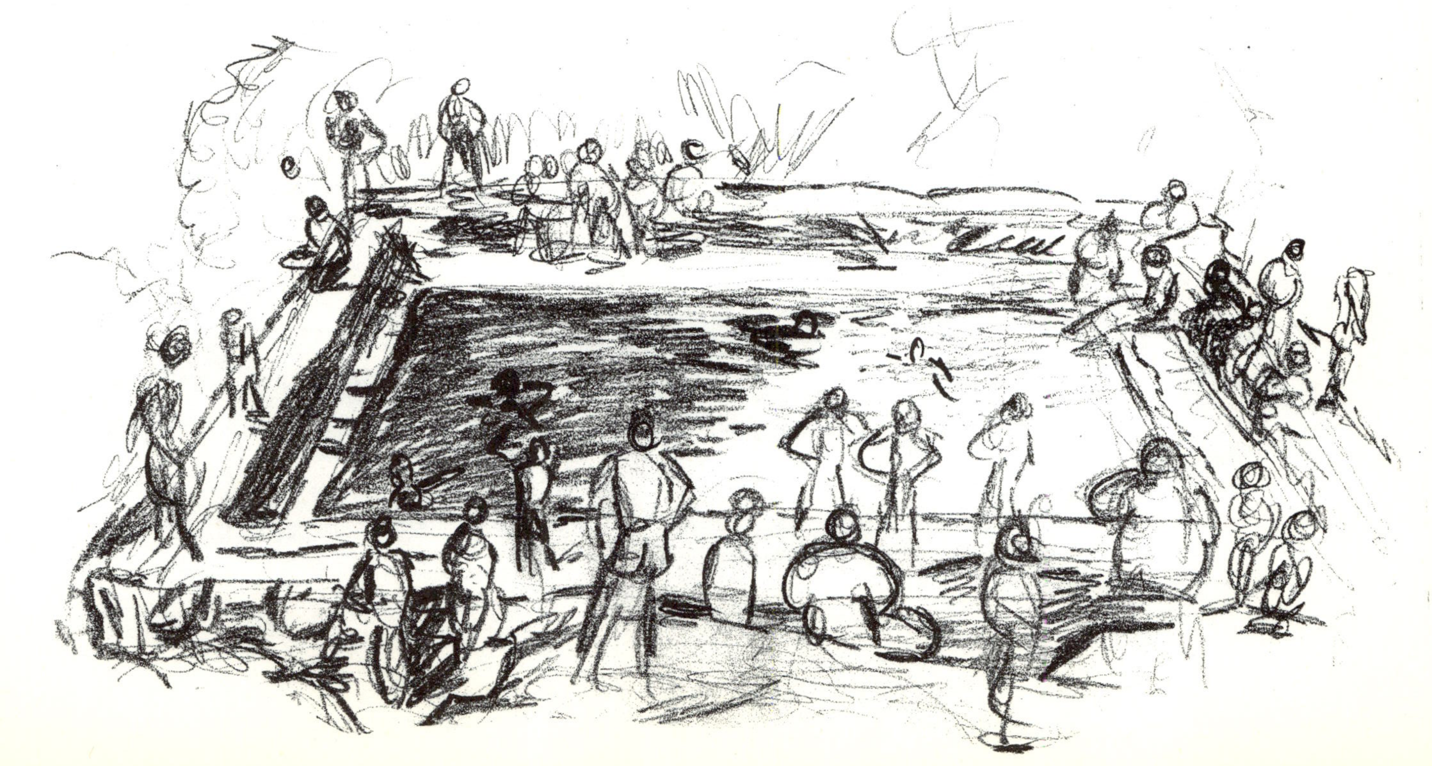

THE ISRAELI SETTLEMENT ON THE NEXT HILL IS CONSTANTLY EXPANDING.

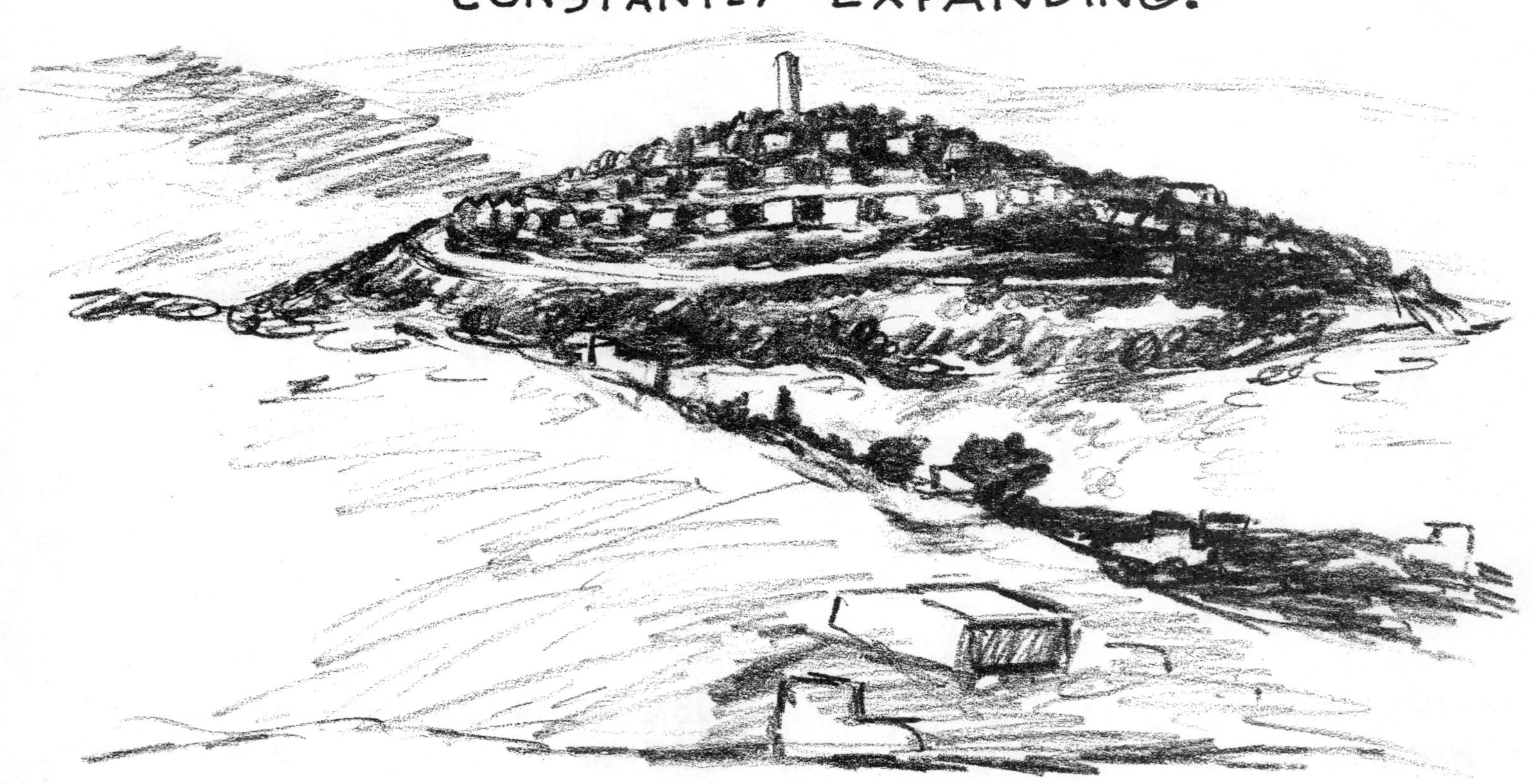

RECENTLY A PALESTINIAN SUED A SETTLER FOR TAKING OVER LAND TO WHICH THE PALESTINIAN HELD A GENERATIONS OLD DEED. THE JUDGE RULED THAT BECAUSE THE ARAB WAS NOT GROWING ANYTHING ON THAT LAND, AN OLD LAW FROM THE DAYS OF THE TURKISH EMPIRE ALLOWED THE SETTLER TO KEEP THE LAND. THAT'S ADVERSE POSSESION, FAIR ENOUGH, BUT NO ONE CAN IMAGINE AN ARAB TAKING LAND FROM THE ISRAELIS IN THIS WAY. IRONICALLY, MANY OF THE YOUNG MEN IN DIRIBZIA WORK IN THE SETTLEMENTS. THEY TOLD ME THAT THE SETTLEMENTS ARE LARGELY EMPTY, BECAUSE, LIKE THE PALESTINIAN MIDDLE CLASS, WEALTHIER SETTLERS PREFER TO SIT THE WAR OUT SOME PLACE **ELSE.**

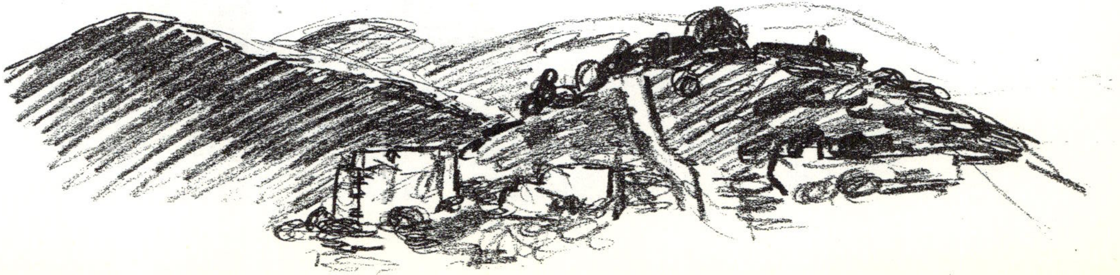

DIRIBZIA AND A NUMBER OF OTHER VILLAGES
ARE IN TROUBLE BECAUSE OF AN INCIDENT
WHICH TOOK PLACE AT A CHECKPOINT
ON THE ROAD CONNECTING
DIRIBZIA TO RAMALLAH.
SOLDIERS SHOT SOME
VILLAGERS, AND SOON
AFTER, SOME
SOLDIERS WERE
SHOT IN AN ACT OF
RETALIATION.
ISRAEL
RESPONDED
BY CLOSING THE
ROAD BETWEEN
DIRIBZIA AND
RAMALLAH.

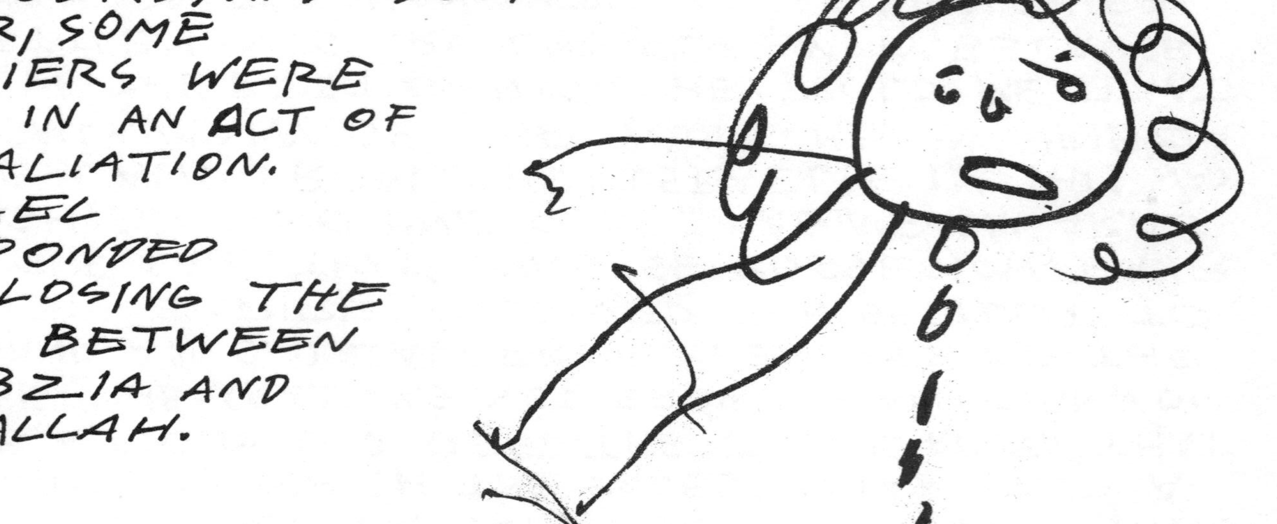

THAT, ALONG WITH THE FACT THAT RAMALLAH IS UNDER CURFEW, EFFECTIVELY ISOLATES DIRIBZIA FROM THE OUTSIDE WORLD.
HIGHSCHOOL AND COLLEGE STUDENTS HAVE TO SNEAK THROUGH THE MOUNTAINS TO GET TO CLASS IN RAMALLAH.
FARMERS CANNOT GET GRAIN FOR THEIR LIVESTOCK.
THIS COMPARITIVELY PROSPEROUS VILLAGE MAY SOON BE REDUCED TO POVERTY.

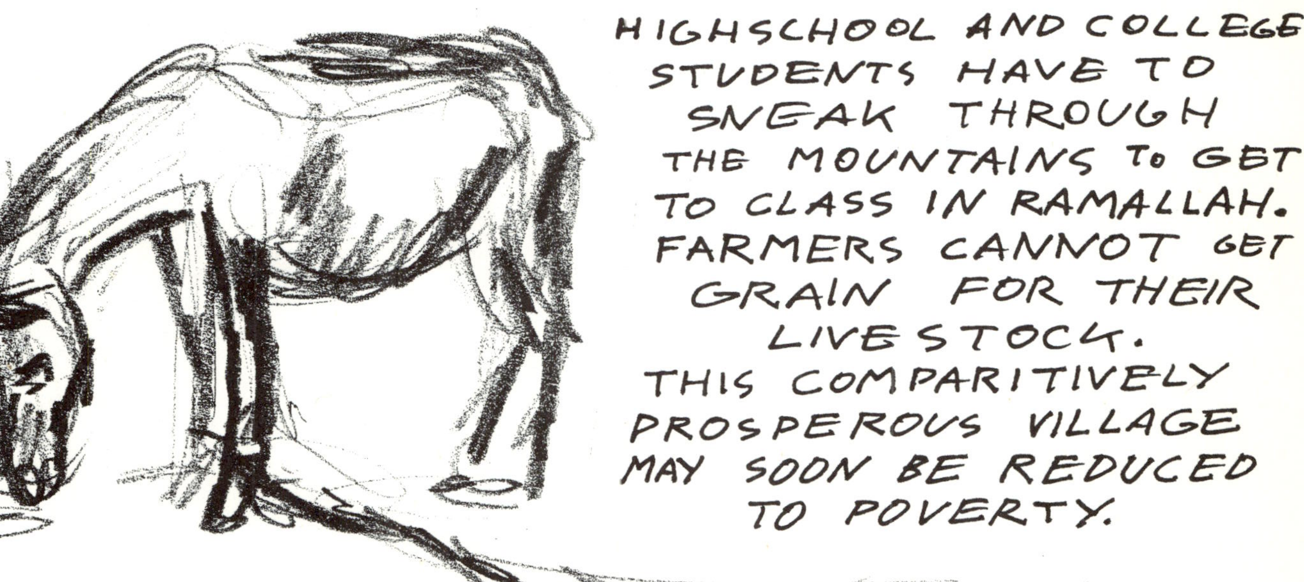

WOMEN

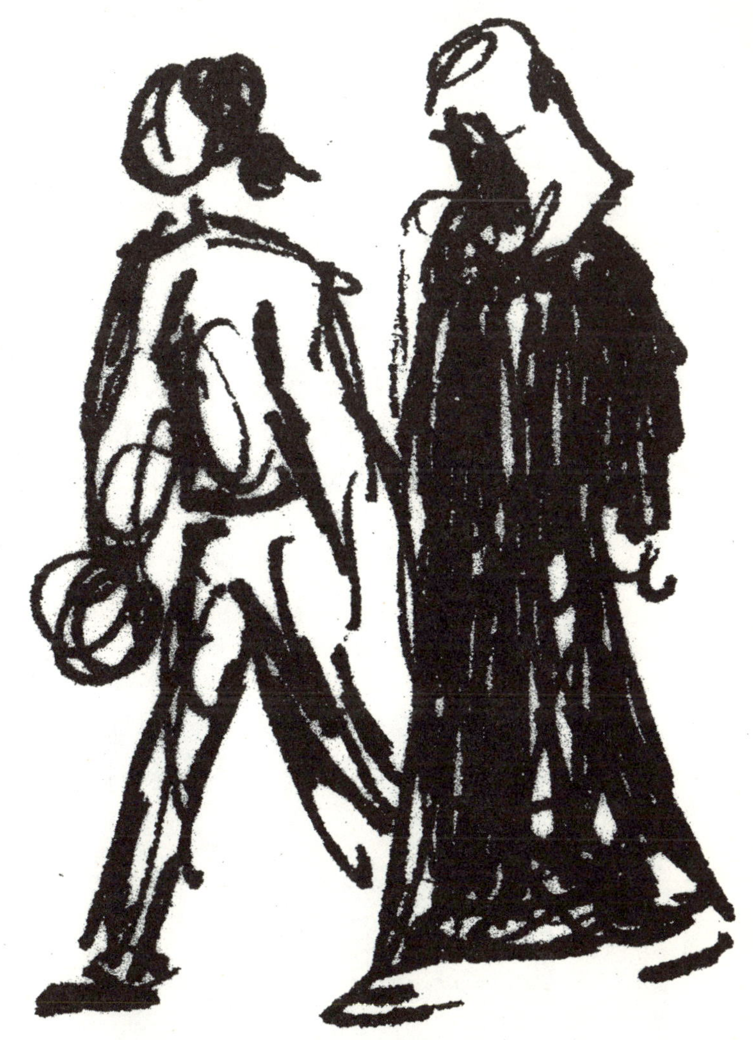

COVERED AND OTHERWISE

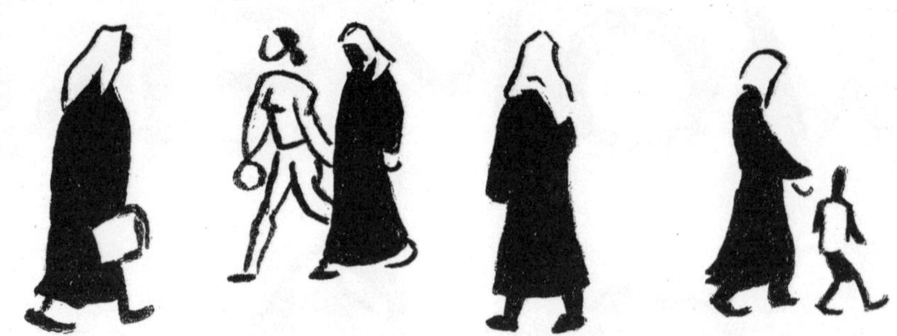

I DID NOT DRAW MANY PORTRAITS OF PALESTINIAN WOMEN WHILE IN JERUSALEM. GIRLS DID NOT RUN UP AND ASK TO BE DRAWN AS THE BOYS DID. AMERICANS HAD ADVISED ME NOT TO DRAW WOMEN. THESE SKETCHES WERE DRAWN FROM A THIRD STORY WINDOW.

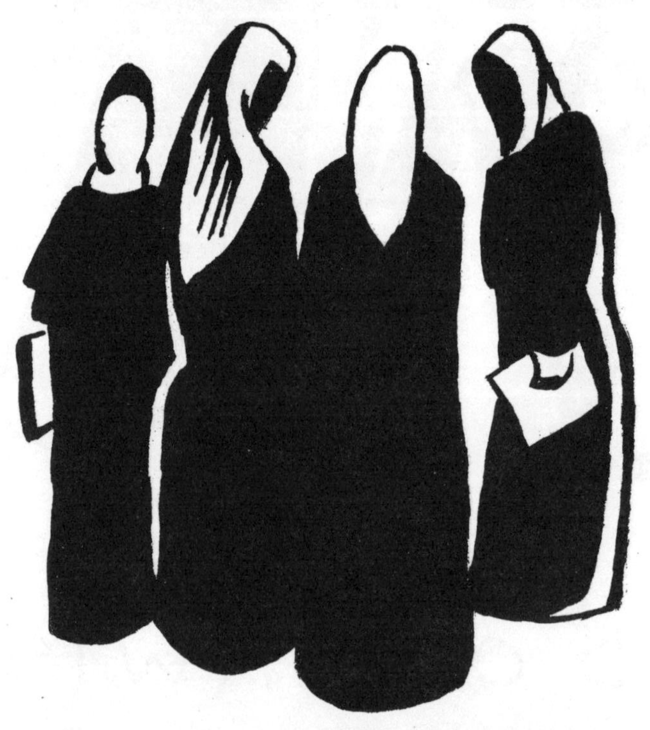

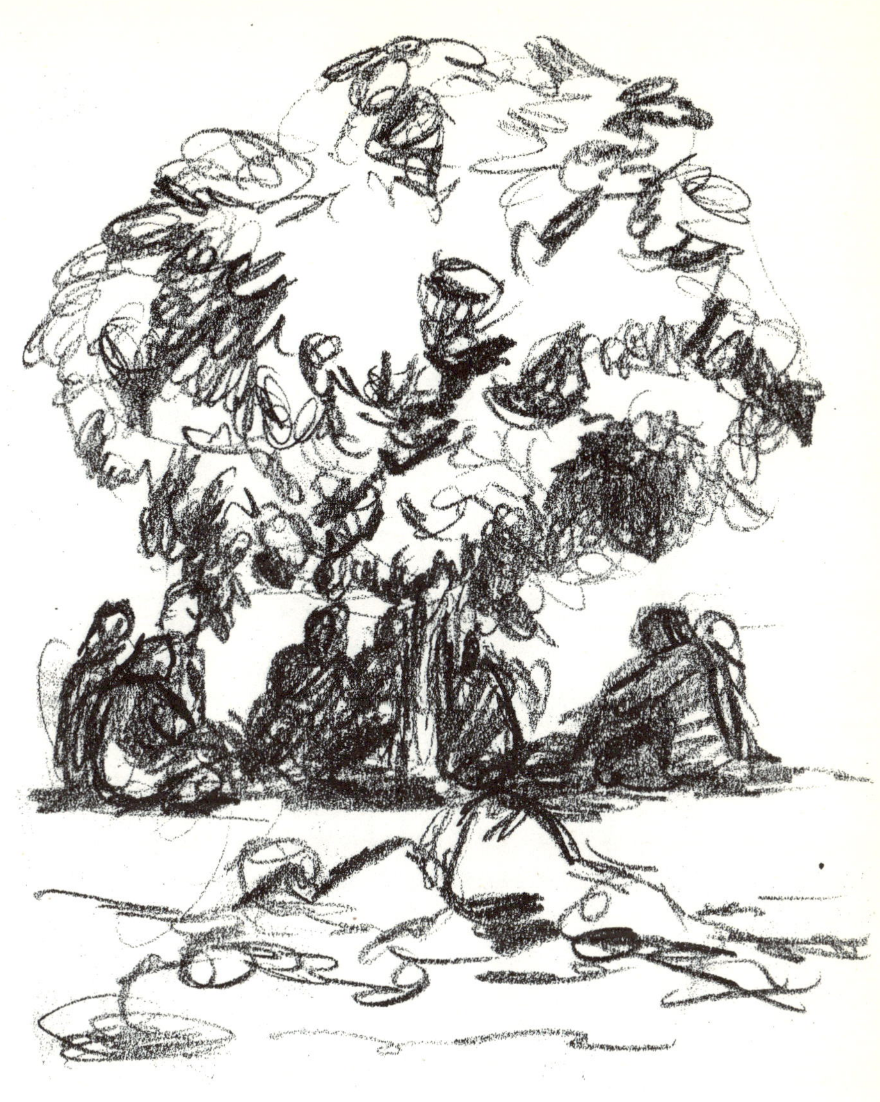

IT WAS NOT UNTIL I'D BEEN TEACHING IN DIRIBZIA FOR A WEEK, AND PEOPLE BEGAN TO INVITE ME INTO THEIR HOMES, THAT I BEGAN TO DRAW THE WOMEN OF THE VILLAGE.

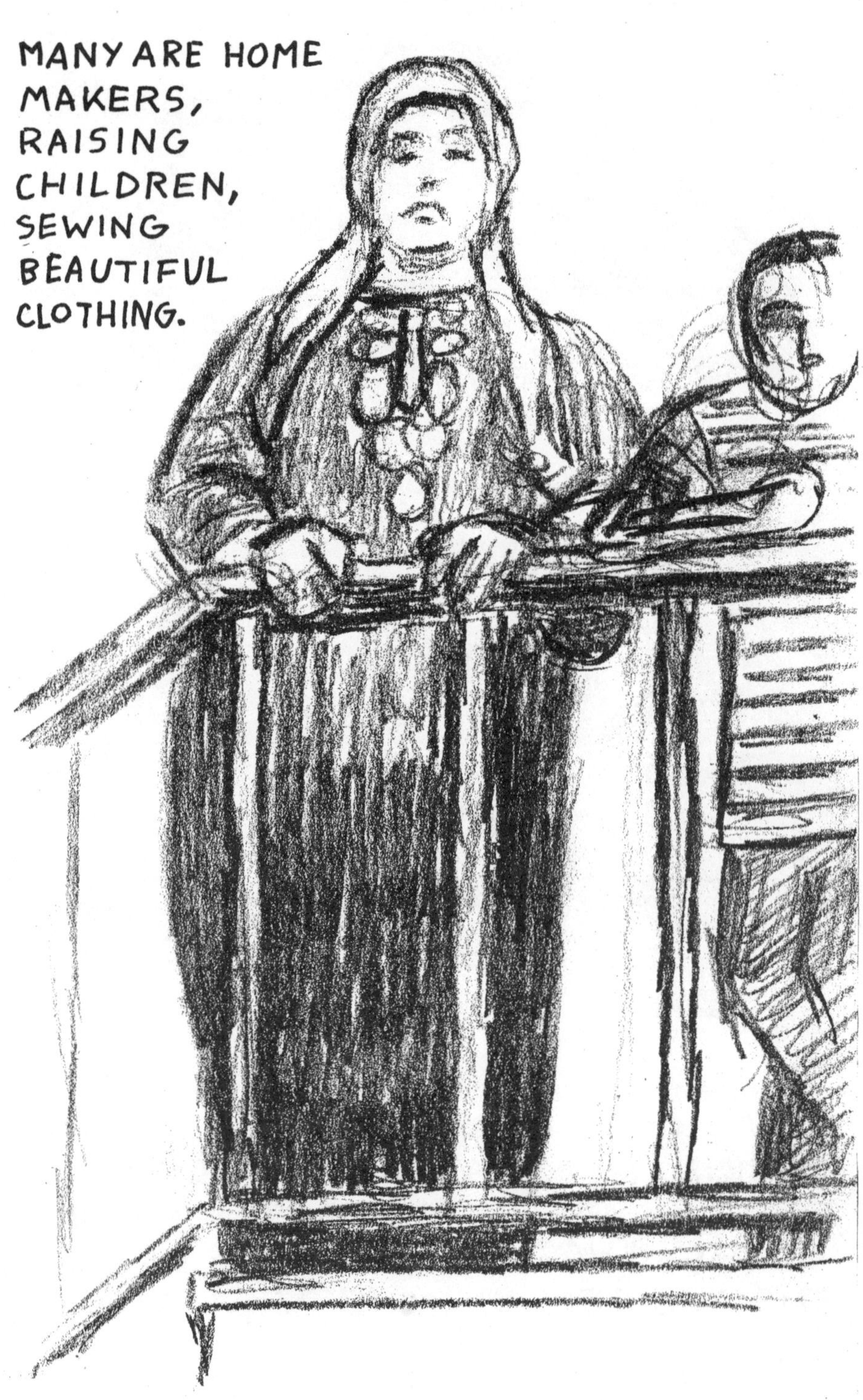
MANY ARE HOME MAKERS, RAISING CHILDREN, SEWING BEAUTIFUL CLOTHING.

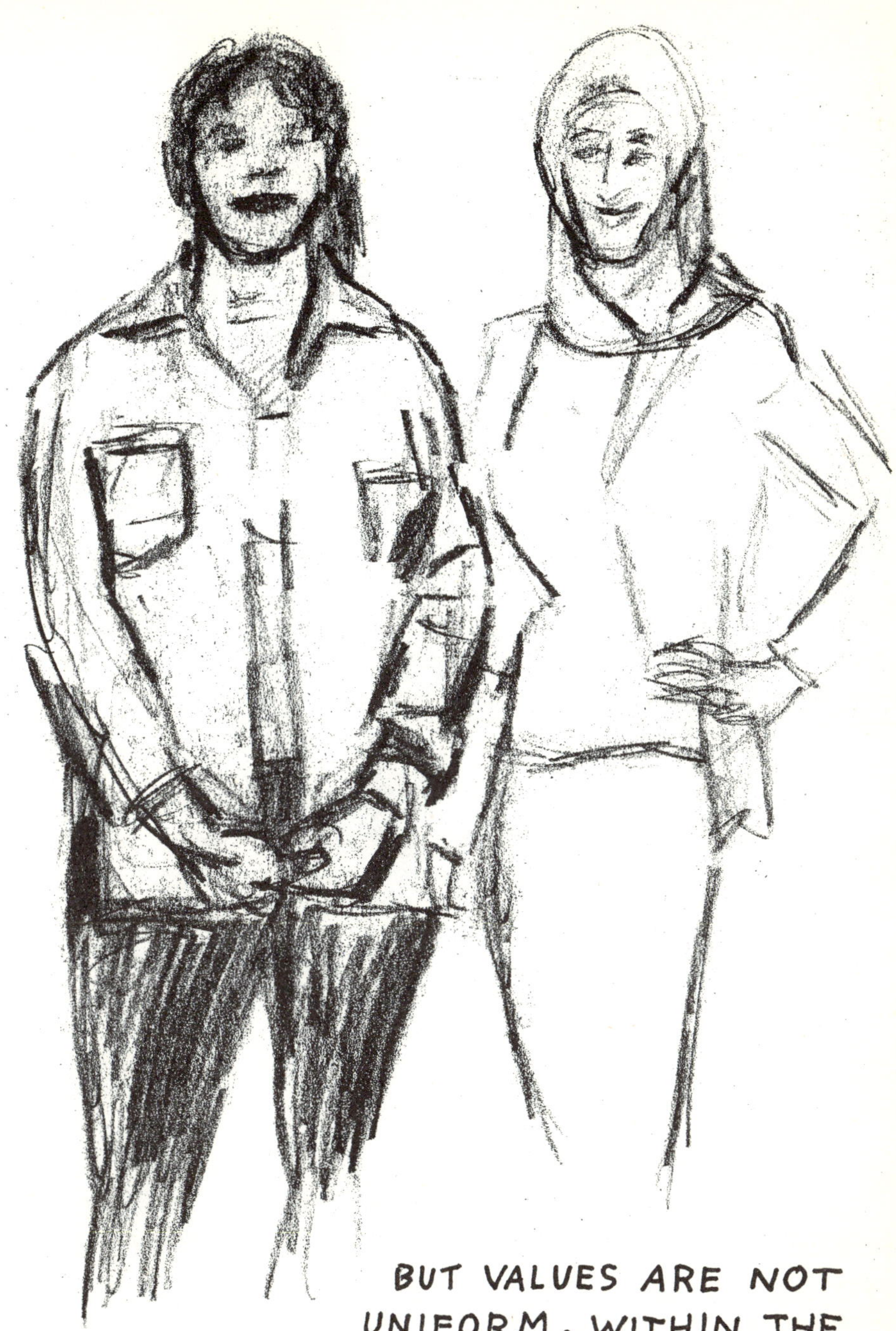

BUT VALUES ARE NOT UNIFORM. WITHIN THE SAME PEER GROUP THERE ARE DIFFERENT ATTITUDES TOWARD TRADITION AND RELIGION.

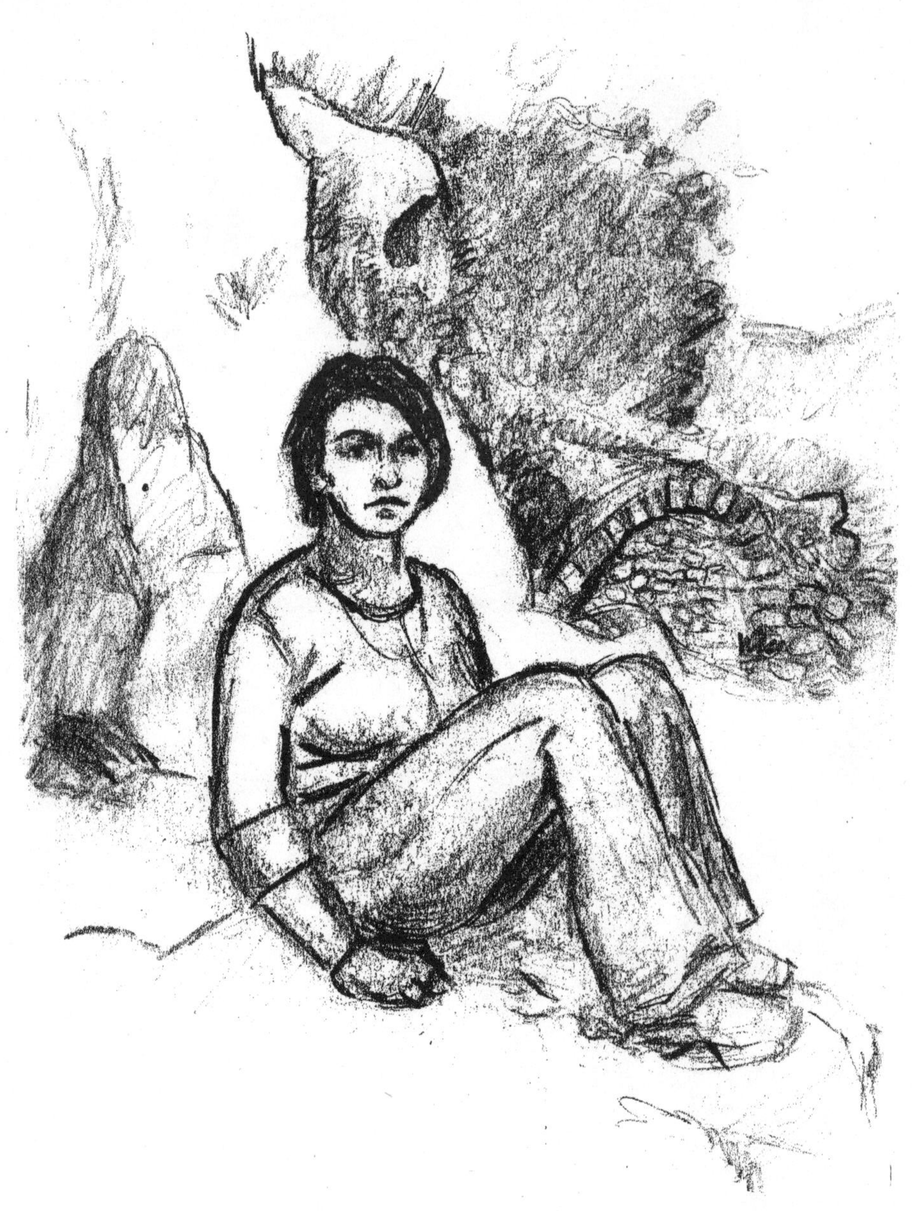

"IT IS VERY BORING TO HAVE A TANK IN FRONT OF YOUR HOUSE. YOU CANNOT GO OUTSIDE. BECAUSE THERE IS A TANK. GIRLS IN EUROPE GET TO GO TO DISCOS."

LEILA KAMAL

"OUR VILLAGE IS BEAUTIFUL, BUT MAYBE IS NOT SO BEAUTIFUL. I DON'T WANT TO GROW UP TO BE ONE OF THESE VILLAGE WOMEN WHO MARRIES AND COVERS HER HEAD AND BAKES BREAD FOR HER HUSBAND AND HAS EVERY YEAR ANOTHER CHILD."

NADIA KAMAL

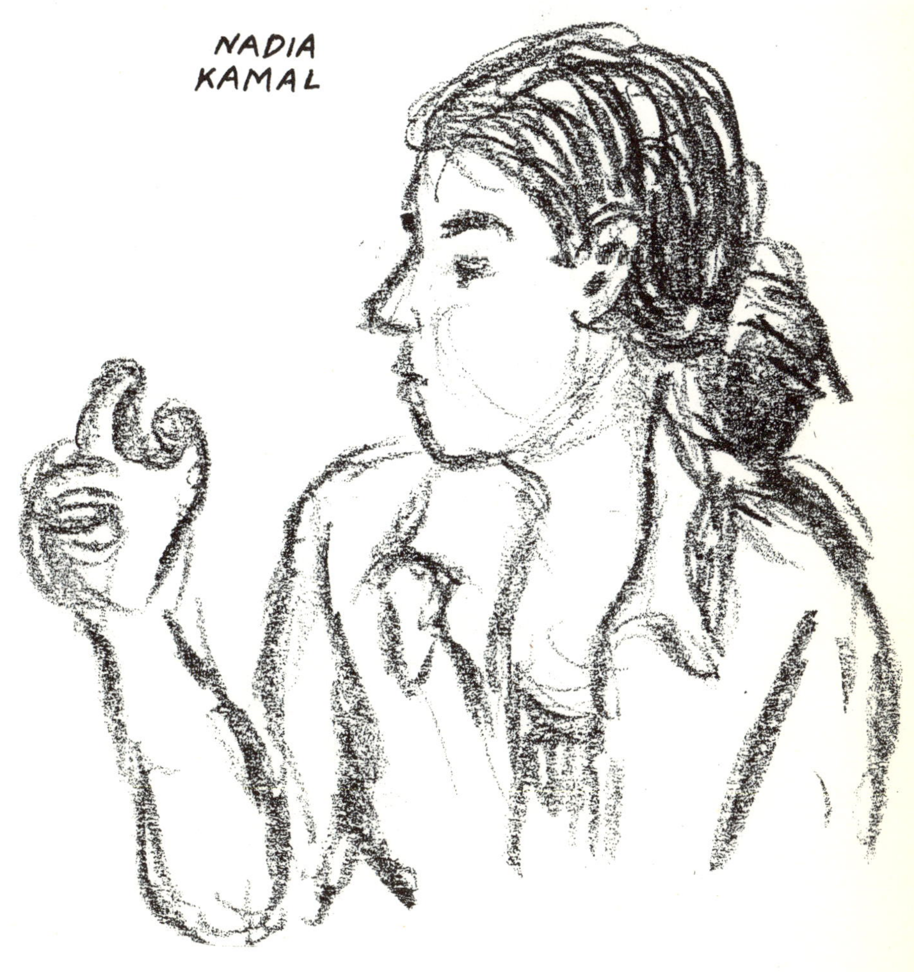

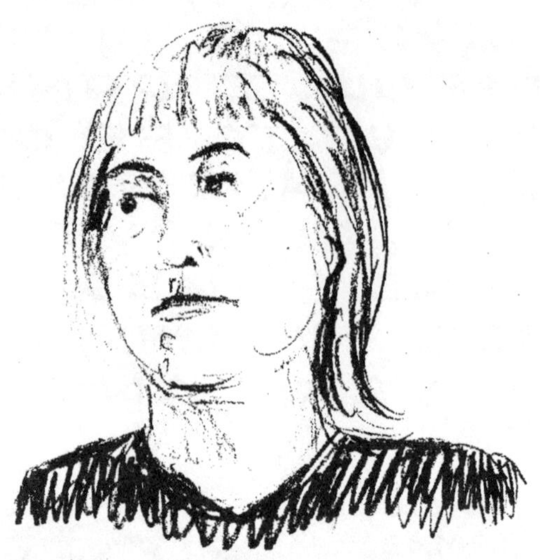

THESE TWO WOMEN ARE BOTH MARRIED TO THE SAME MAN.

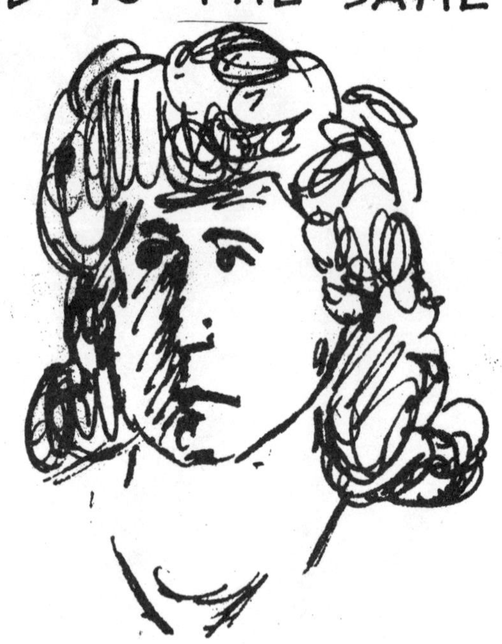

WHEN RIVKA CAME TO DIRIBZIA, THE VILLAGE MATRIARCHS APPROVED OF THE FACT THAT SHE COVERED HER HAIR AND SHOULDERS, AND WOULD NOT TOUCH MEN. THEY ASKED HER "ARE YOU AN ARAB?"

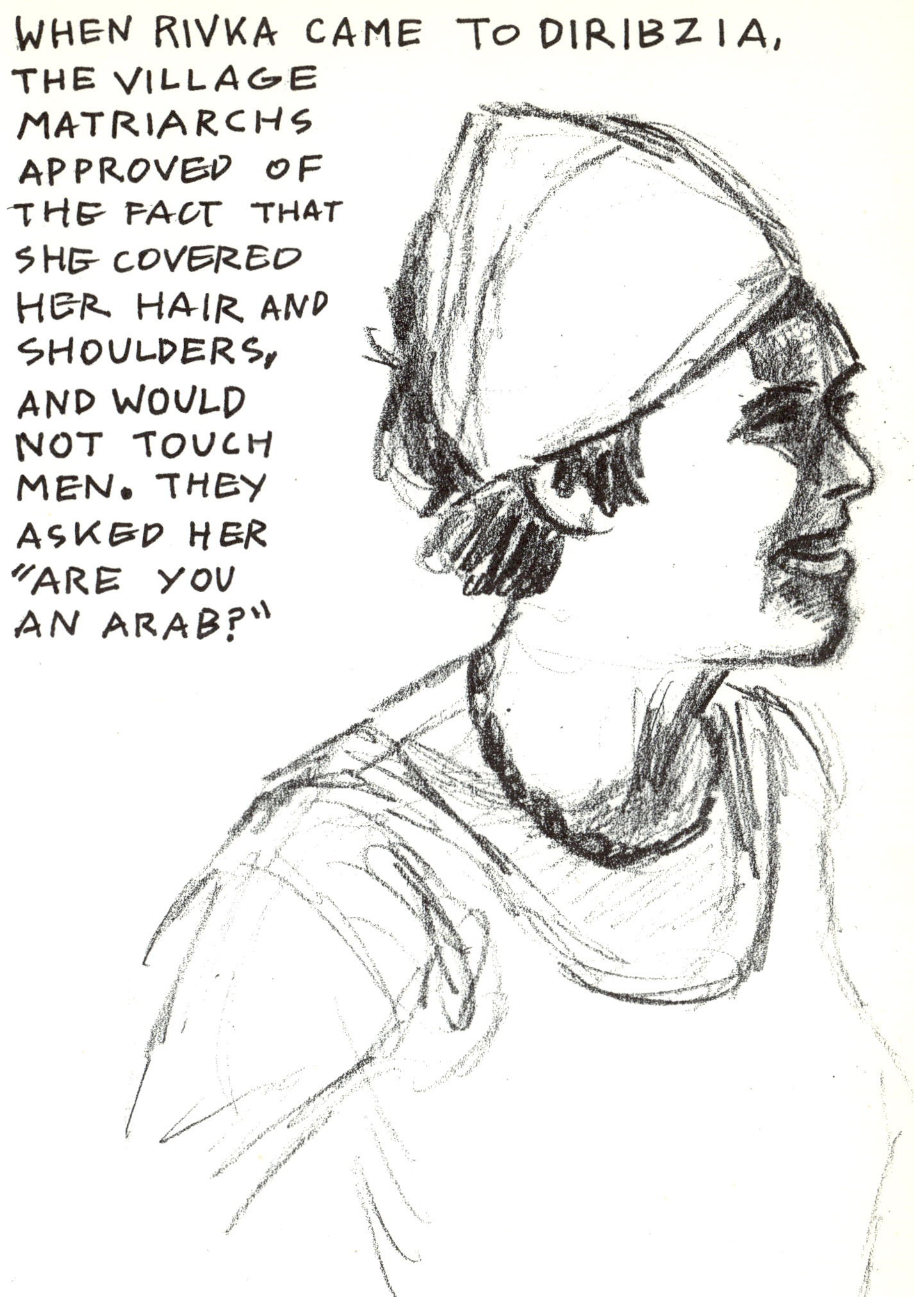

BUT RIVKA WAS AN ORTHODOX JEW.

THE HOSPITAL

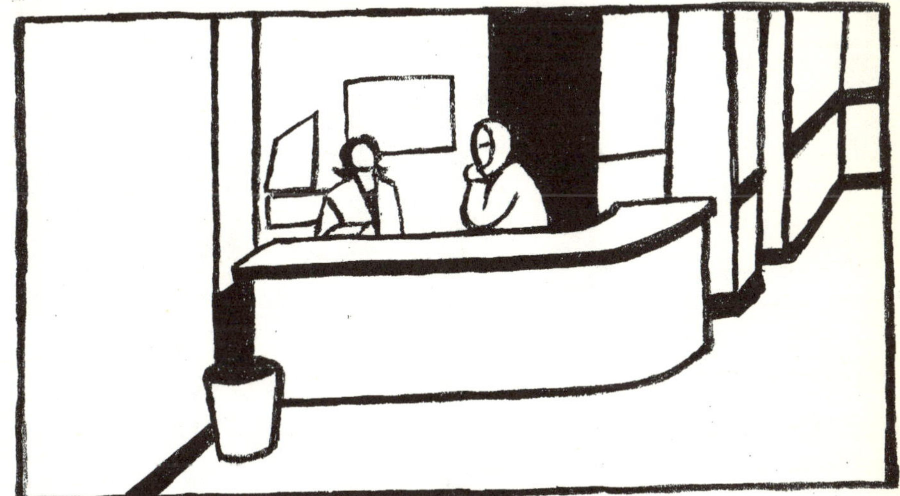

IN RAMALLAH

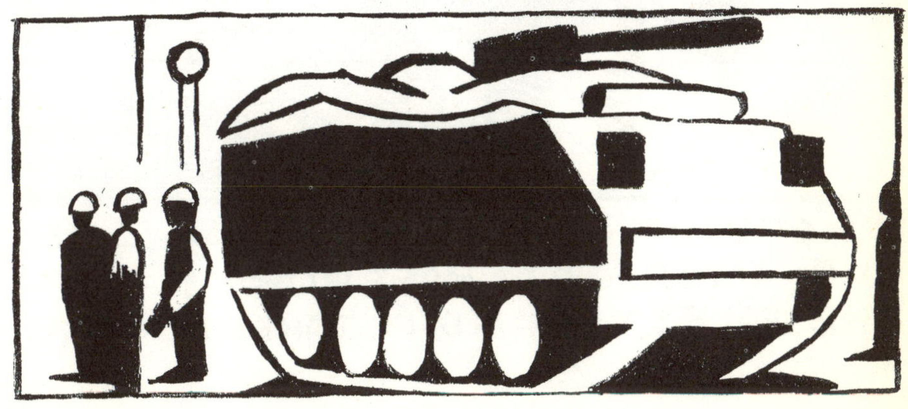

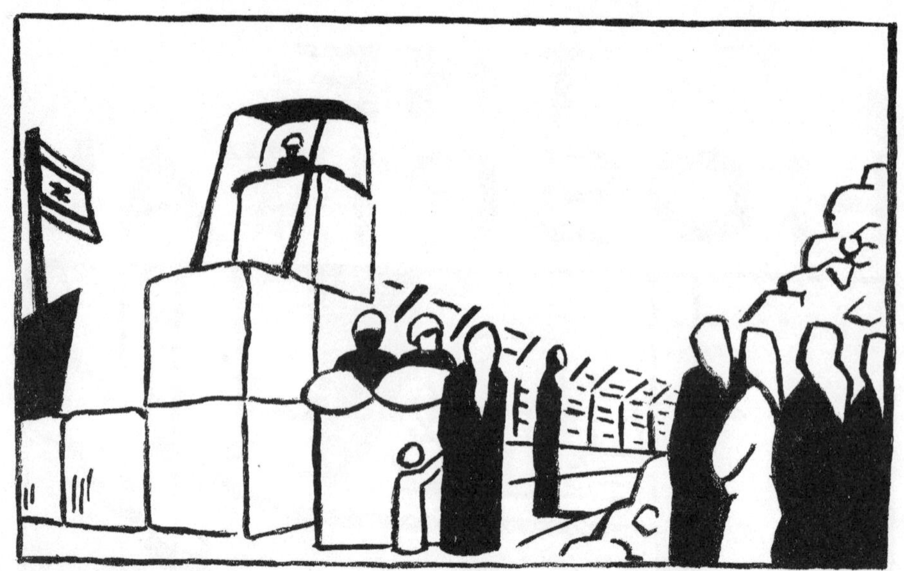

TO GET INTO RAMALLAH, WE HAVE TO PASS THROUGH QALANDIA CHECKPOINT. PEOPLE WAIT FOR HOURS IN THE HOT SUN.

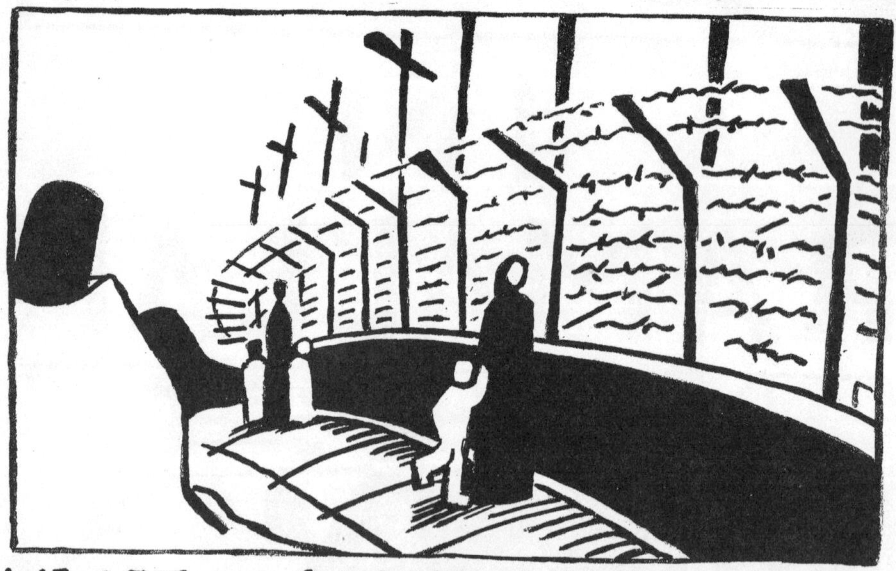

WE GET IN QUICKLY BECAUSE OF OUR AMERICAN PASSPORTS. FOR THE PALESTINIANS IT TAKES LONGER.

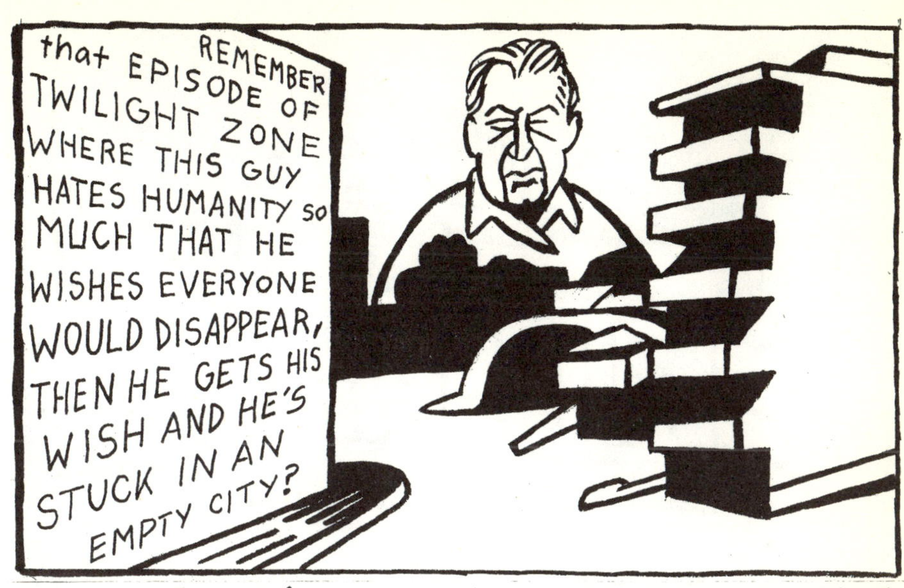

WELL, THAT'S WHAT CURFEW IS LIKE IN RAMALLAH. ANY PALESTINIAN SEEN OUT ON THE STREET CAN BE SHOT ON SIGHT.

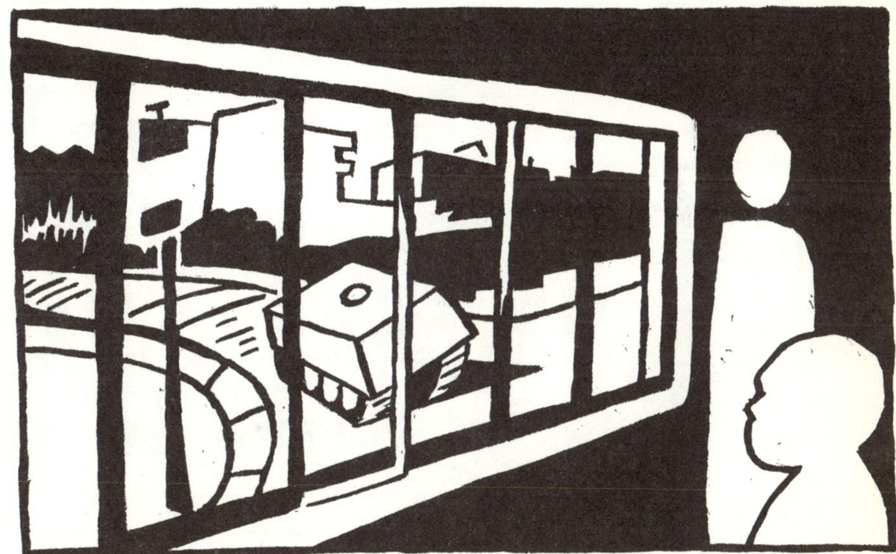

PEOPLE STAY INSIDE. THEY CAN'T GO TO WORK OR SCHOOL. SOCIETY BREAKS DOWN.

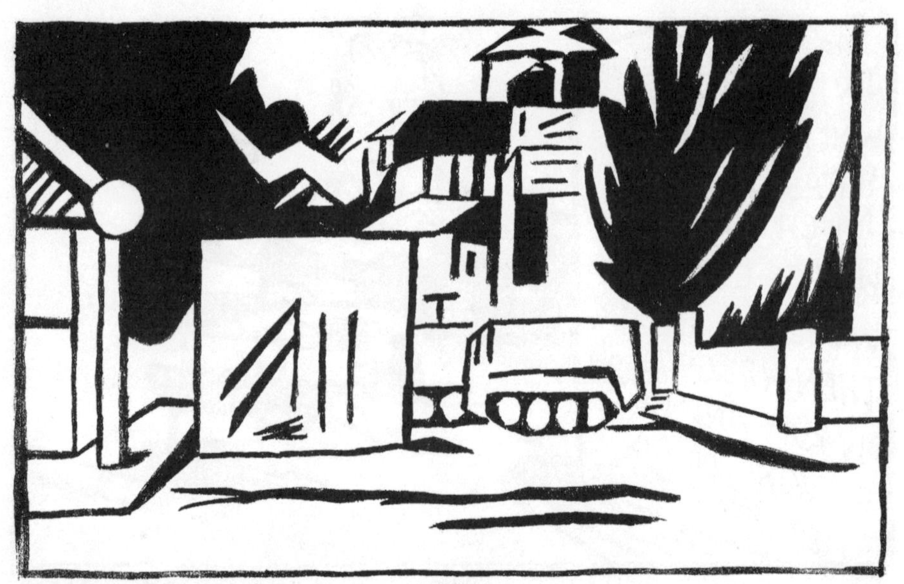

THE STREETS ARE EMPTY, EXCEPT FOR THE TANKS. SILENT, EXCEPT FOR THE OCCASIONAL EXPLOSIONS.

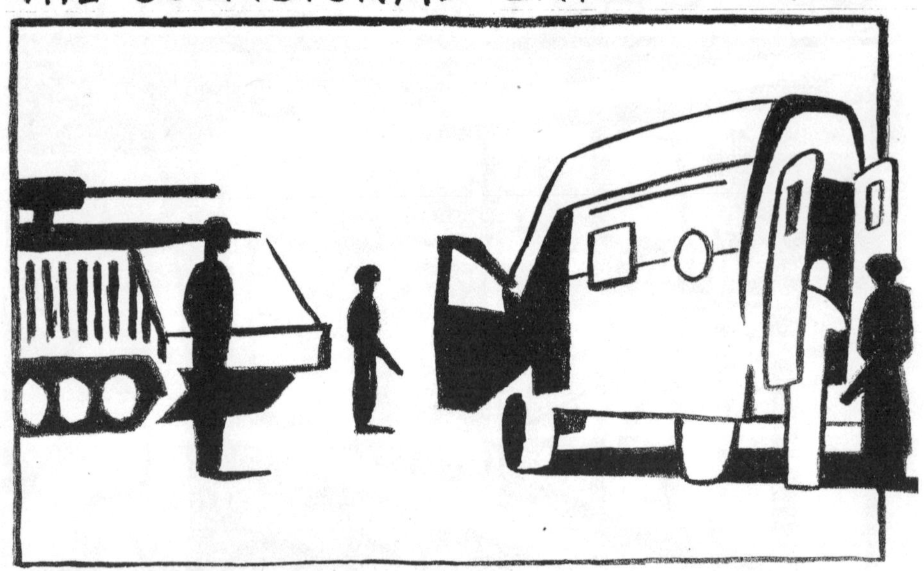

EVERY AMBULANCE IS SEARCHED BEFORE ENTERING THE HOSPITAL, EVEN IF IT CARRIES AN EMERGENCY CASE.

AT THE HOSPITAL, WE MEET THE DOCTOR, THE AMBULANCE DRIVERS, THE HOSPITAL WORKERS, AND A FEW OTHER FOLKS.

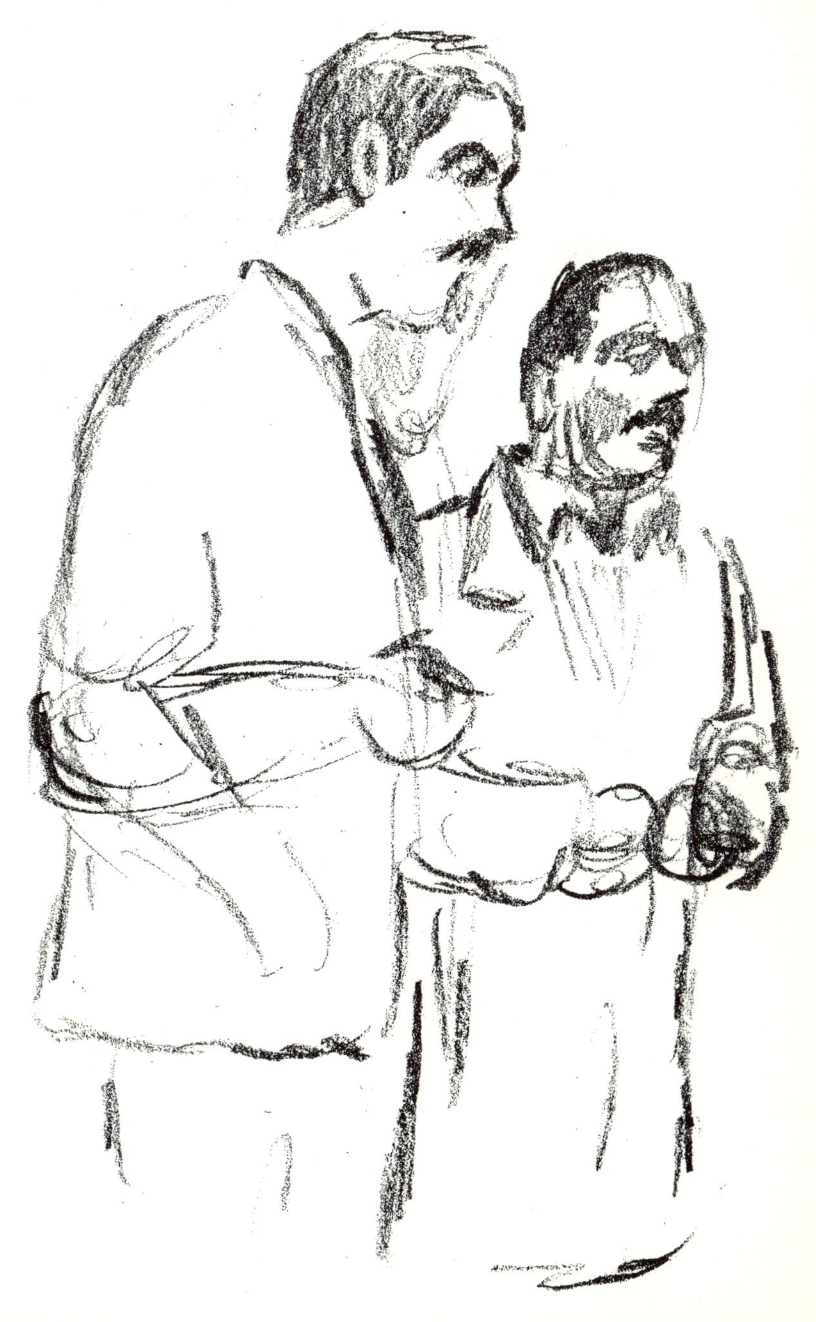

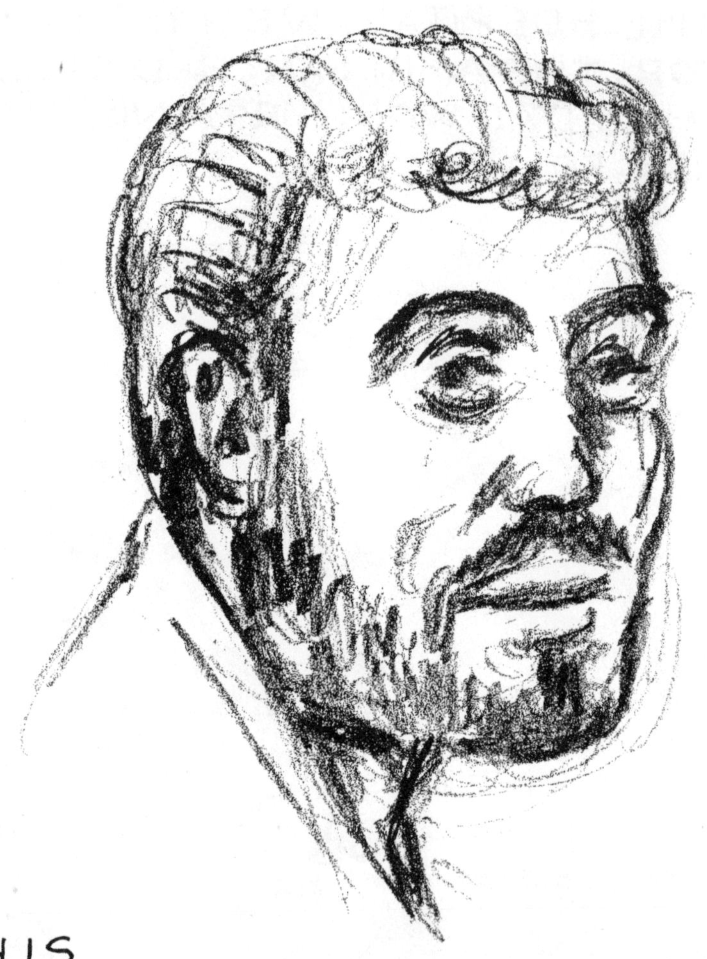

THIS
PALESTINIAN-AMERICAN HOSPITAL WORKER LIVED IN COLORADO. AFTER OSLO, HE CAME BACK TO HELP HIS PEOPLE. HE'S BEEN STAYING AT THE HOSPITAL 24-7 BECAUSE CURFEW WILL NOT LET HIM LEAVE. HE HAS ALSO BEEN TAKING OVER THE SHIFTS OF OTHER HOSPITAL WORKERS WHO ARE TRAPPED IN THEIR HOMES.

THIS MAN BROUGHT A FRIEND TO THE HOSPITAL AFTER THE ISRAELIS BLEW UP THE FRIEND'S HOUSE. NOW, BECAUSE OF CURFEW, HE HAS NOT BEEN ABLE TO LEAVE THE HOSPITAL FOR MANY DAYS. AT LEAST HIS FRIEND HAS COMPANY.

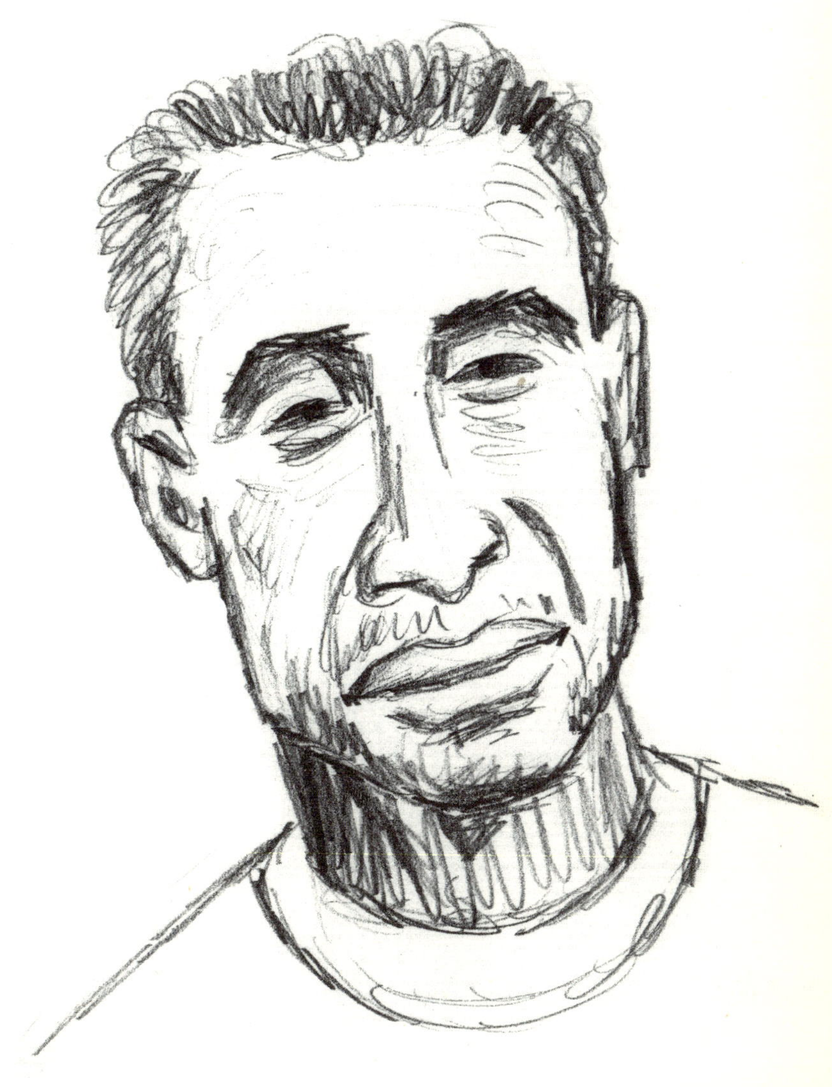

THE HEAD DOCTOR DID THIS SKETCH OF ME

HE SAID THAT HE USED TO BE AN ARTIST.

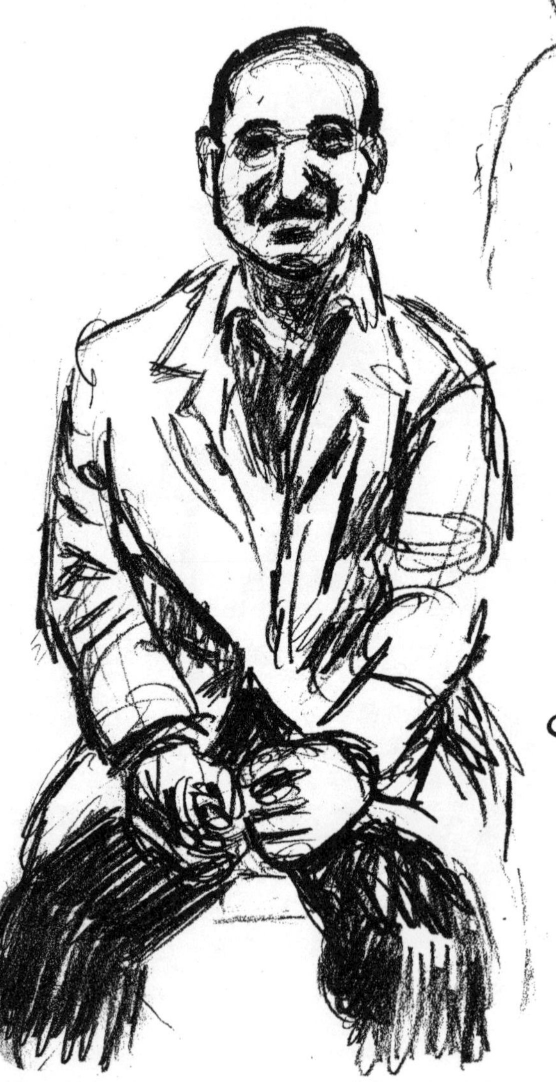

BUT HIS DRAWINGS WERE POLITICAL AND THE ISRAELIS CONFISCATED THEM.

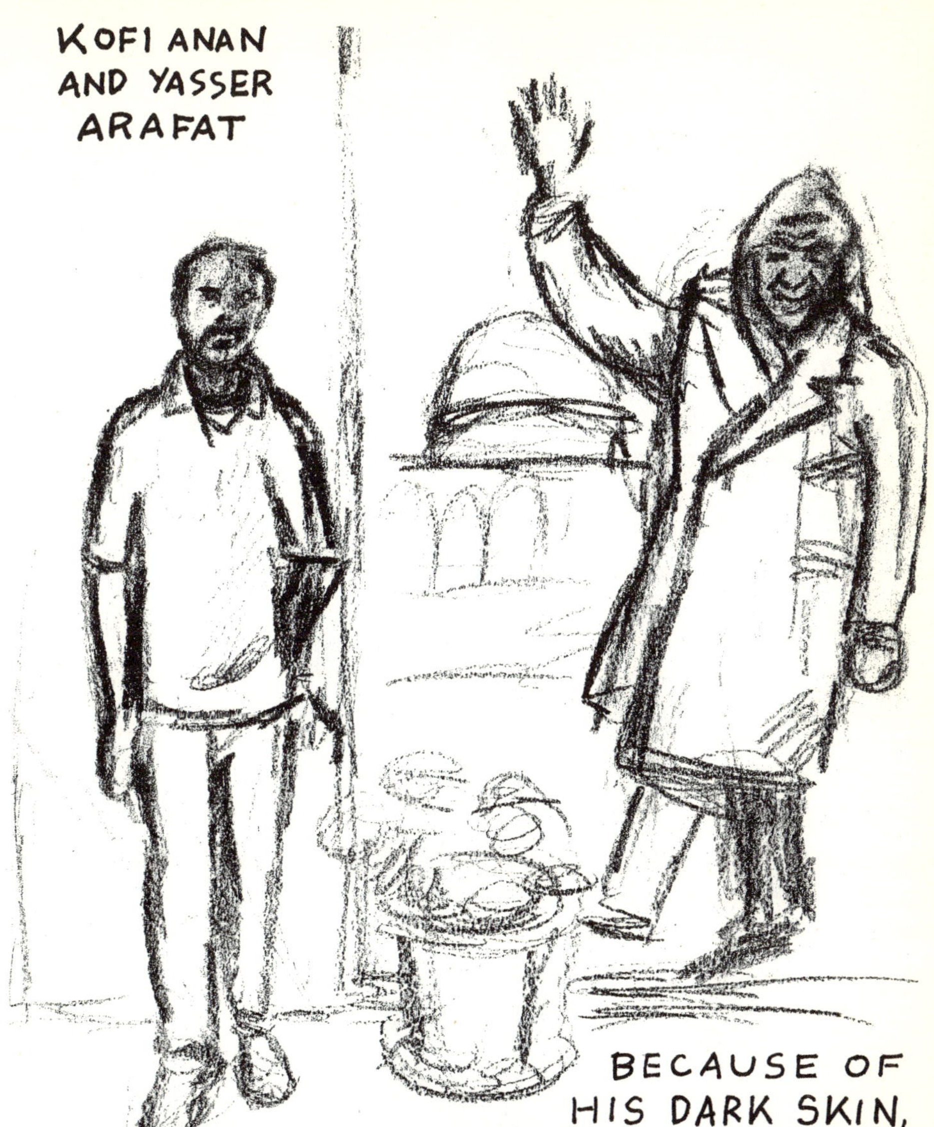

BECAUSE OF HIS DARK SKIN, THEY CALL THIS JANITOR KOFI ANAN. HERE'S KOFI ANAN POSING IN FRONT OF A PICTURE OF HIS HERO YASSER ARAFAT. BEFORE WE JUDGE THIS TOO HARSHLY, LET'S REMEMBER THAT GEORGE WASHINGTON OWNED SLAVES AND THAT DIDN'T KEEP HIS FACE OFF THE DOLLAR BILL.

2280 PALESTINIANS HAVE DIED IN THE INTIFADA SO FAR! EVERYONE LOSES A FATHER OR A BROTHER! WHEN THIS HAPPENS TO A CHILD, THE CHILD NEVER FORGETS! AND SO, WHAT THE IS-RAELI CALLS THE TERRORISM IS BECAUSE OF WHAT THE ISRAELI DOES TO US!

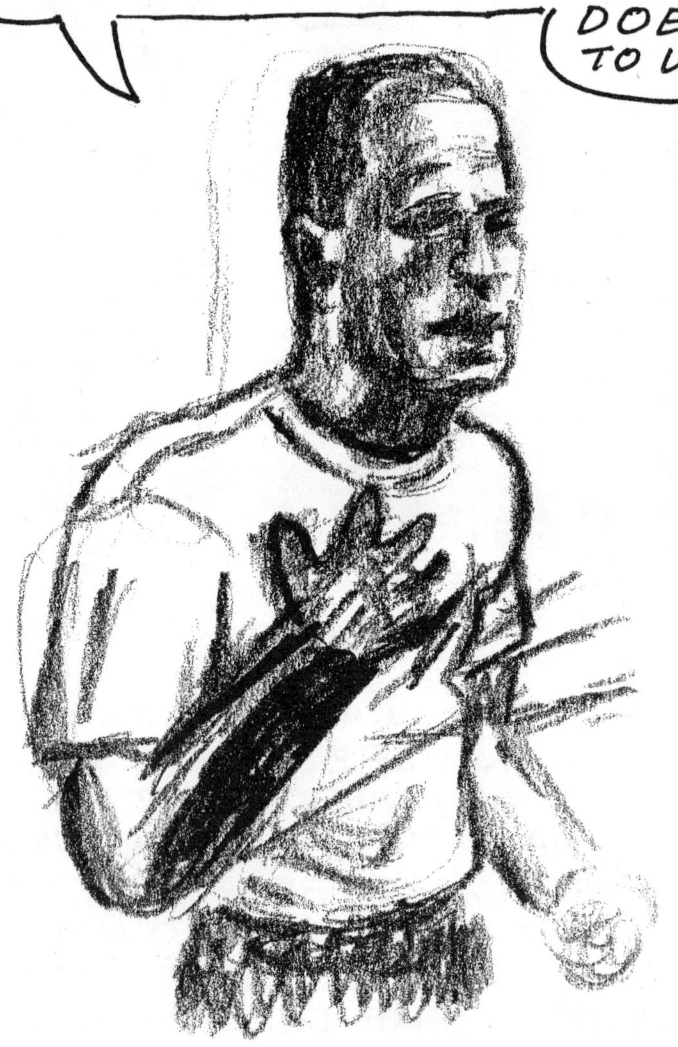

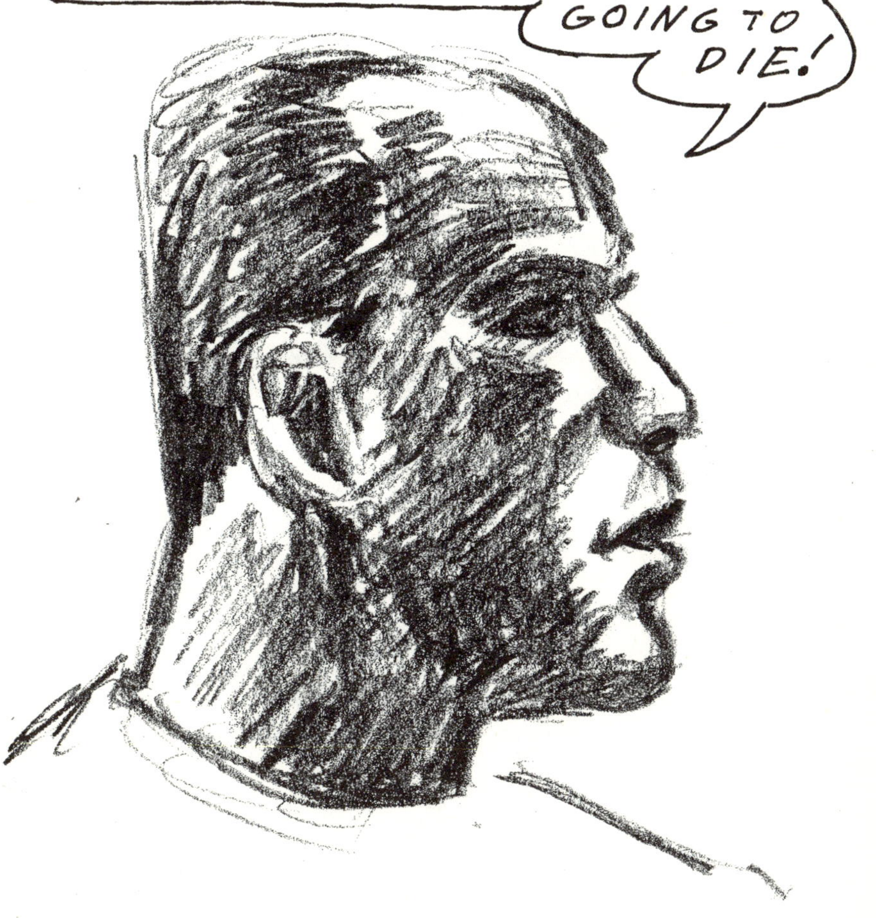
I SAID TO A MUSLIM MAN "ALLAH IS NOT THE GOD." HE SAID "ALLAH IS THE GOD." I SAID "YOU ARE WRONG. ALLAH IS NOT THE GOD." HE SAID "MAHMOUD, HOW CAN YOU SAY THAT ALLAH IS NOT THE GOD?" I SAID "BECAUSE ONLY ARIEL SHARON CAN BE THE GOD, BECAUSE HE IS THE ONLY ONE WHO CAN DECIDE IF A PERSON IS GOING TO LIVE, OR IF THAT PERSON IS GOING TO DIE!

THE FIRST JOINT OF MAHMOUD'S INDEX FINGER WAS CUT OFF IN PRISON. THE ISRAELIS WERE TRYING TO GET HIM TO SIGN A PAPER AGAINST HIS FRIEND. THEY THREATENED TO CUT OFF ALL HIS FINGERS. HE SAID THEY COULD GO AHEAD AND CUT THEM OFF BUT HE WOULDN'T SIGN. THEY GAVE UP AND LET HIM GO.

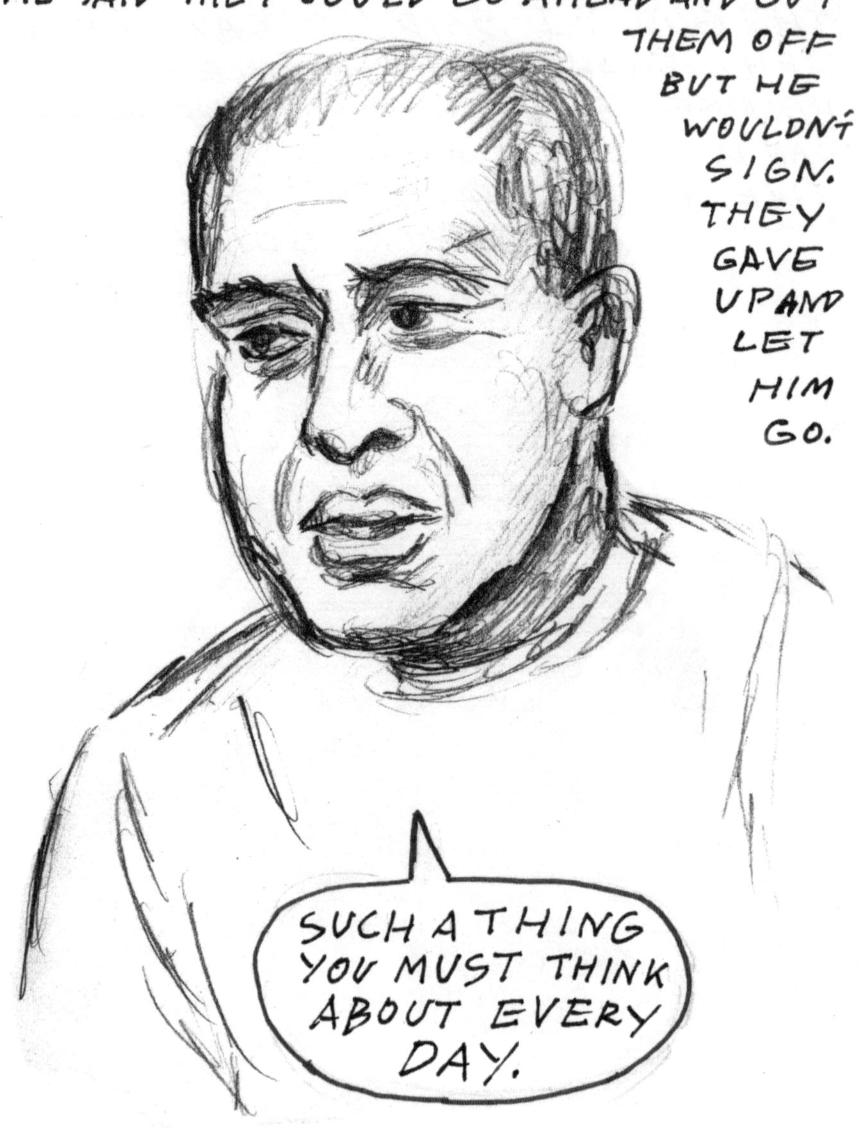

MAHMOUD ORGANIZES EMERGENCY HEALTHCARE FOR THE PALESTINIAN AUTHORITY. HE STILL SUPPORTS YASSER ARAFAT, BUT ALSO RECOGNIZES THAT THERE HAS BEEN CORRUPTION AND FISCAL MIS-MANAGE-MENT IN THE P.A.

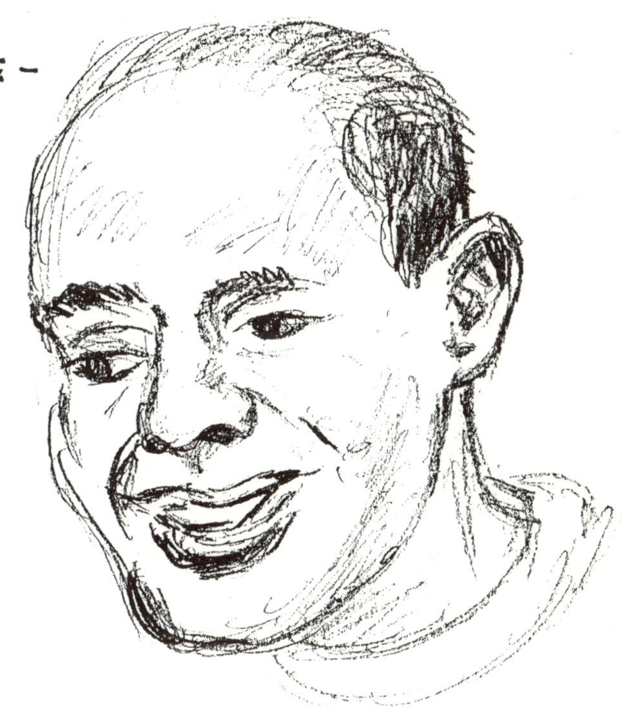

MAHMOUD WAS ALSO IN CHARGE OF OUR SAFETY IN RAMALLAH. AT ONE POINT HE CALLED US UP BY CEL-PHONE TO WARN US NOT TO COME TO THE HOSPITAL TOO SOON BECAUSE THE SOLDIERS WERE BLOWING UP CARS OUT-FRONT.

RIDING THE BUS

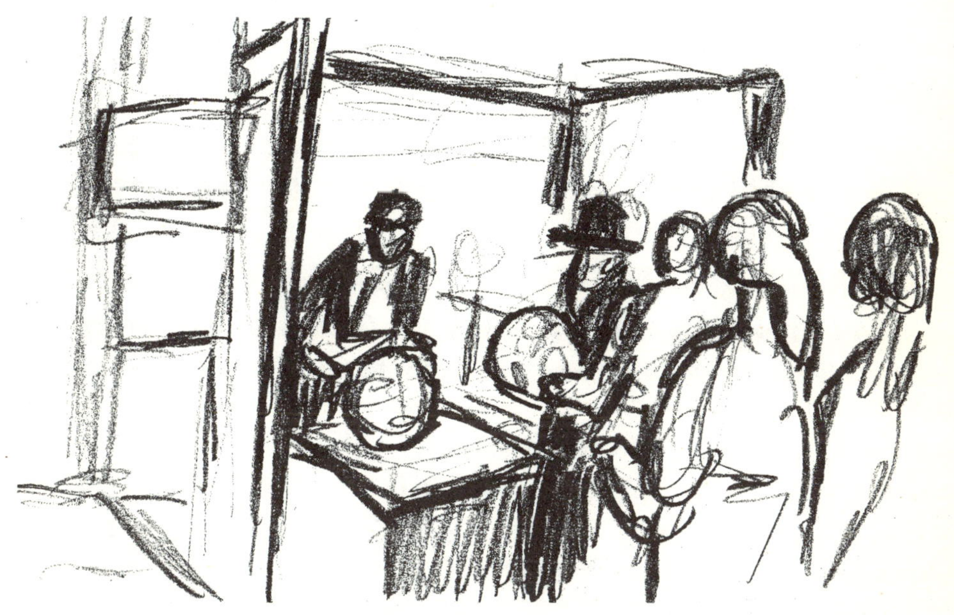

AT NIGHT

THE ARAB CAB DRIVER HAD TO DROP ME OFF A BLOCK AWAY, BECAUSE HE WAS NOT ALLOWED TO DRIVE NEAR THE BUS STATION. PEOPLE HAD TO LINE UP AT THE DOOR TO HAVE THEIR BAGS SEARCHED. I THOUGHT THAT THIS FELT A BIT LIKE THE CHECKPOINTS, ONLY THE ISRAELI KNOWS THAT THE SOLDIER SEARCHING HIM IS ON HIS SIDE AND HE HAS CONFIDENCE HE WON'T BE MISTREATED. INSIDE IT IS AIR CONDITIONED AND IT LOOKS LIKE AN AMERICAN SHOPPING MALL.

AS THE BUS TRAVERSES ISRAELS NEON NIGHT, THE DRIVER HAS HIS RADIO ON. LOUD. POP MUSIC AND AN ISRAELI COMEDIAN SPEAKING HEBREW. I WONDER, ARE HIS JOKES FUNNY? NO ONE SEEMS TO BE LAUGHING.

ARE THE GRIMACES ON THE FACES OF THESE BUS PASSENGERS JUST FATIGUE AT THE END OF A LONG DAYS WORK? OR IS THIS FEAR AND WORRY? IN A COUNTRY WITH TWO NAMES, SOME THINGS HAVE TWO MEANINGS.

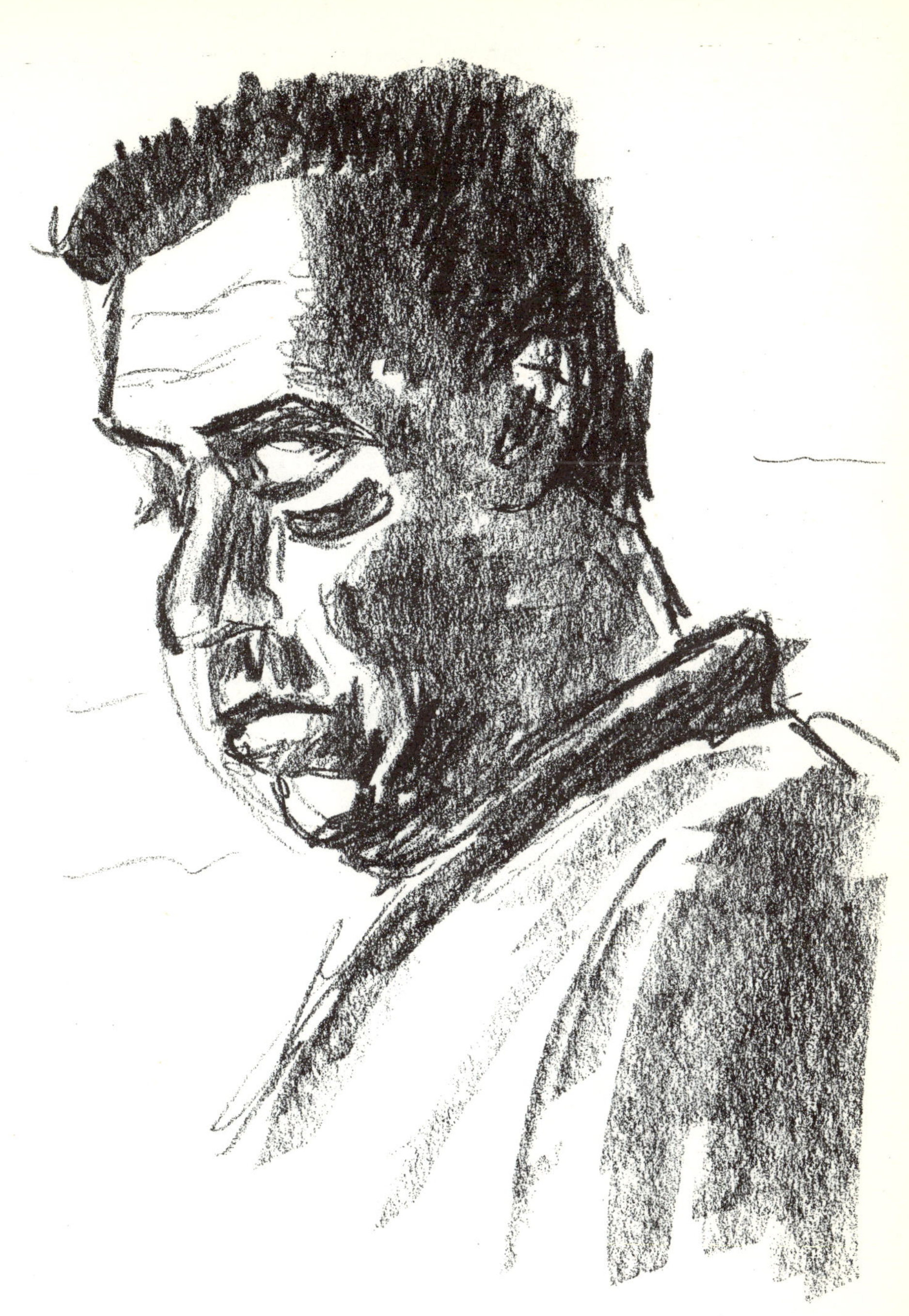

BETWEEN SEPT. 2000 & JULY 2002 350 CIVILIANS WERE KILLED IN ATTACKS ON ISRAELI TARGETS.
—AMNESTY INTERNATIONAL

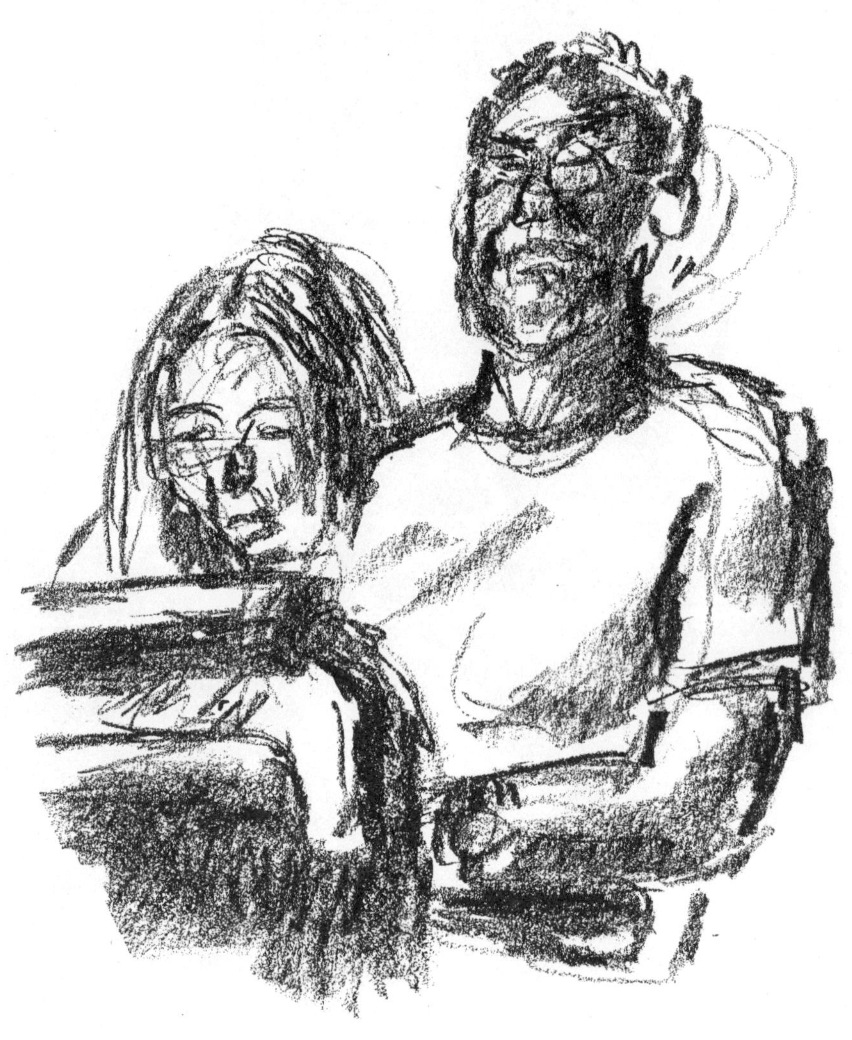

THE BUS IS A TARGET.

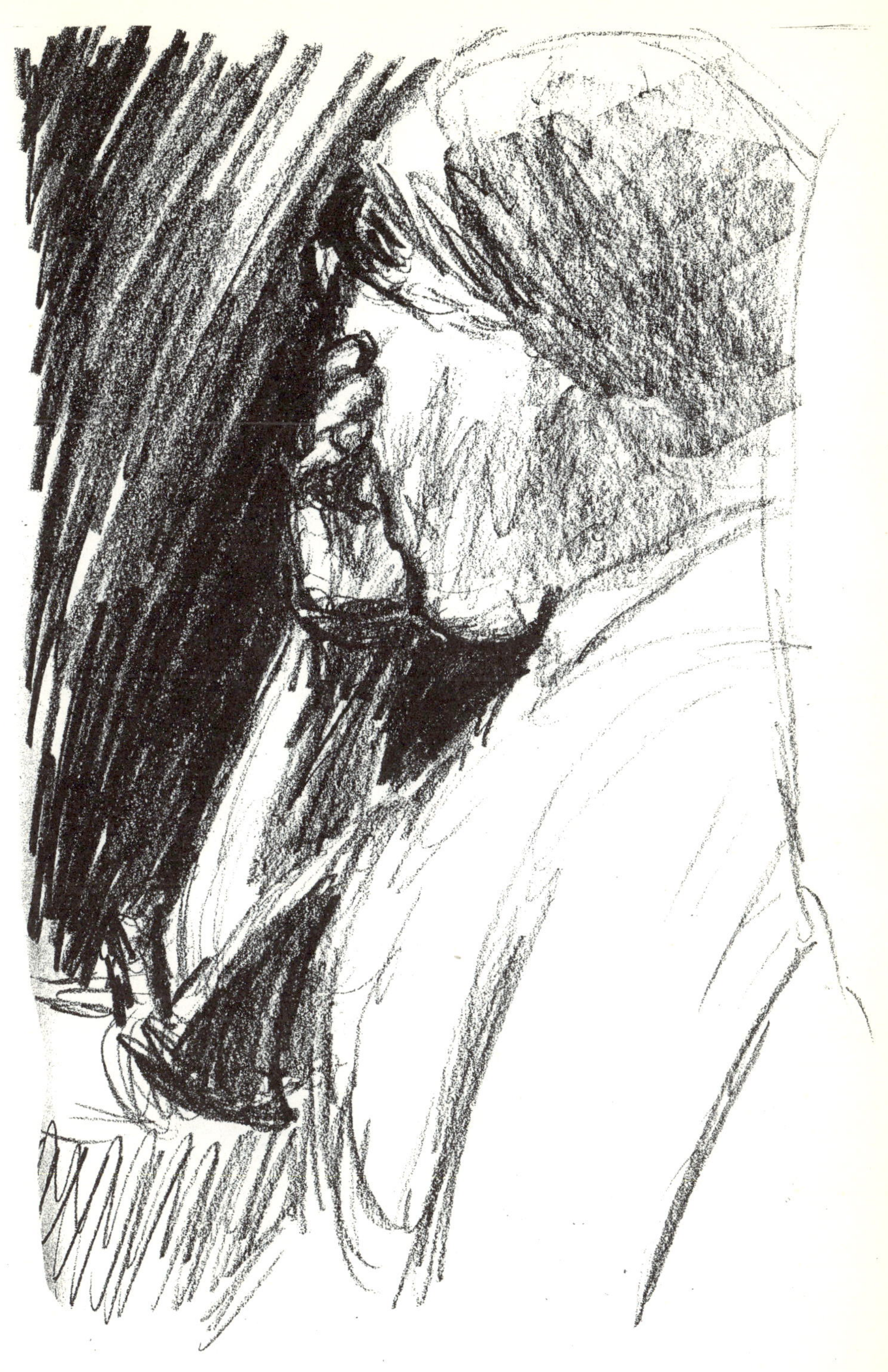

IN THE END, YOU HAVE TO GIVE THEM CREDIT FOR RIDING THESE BUSSES. LAST FALL, THE SHOOTING OF 12 PEOPLE BY WASHINGTON D.C.'S INFAMOUS SNIPER BROUGHT THE CAPITAL TO A STAND-STILL. WE AMERICANS COULD LEARN A LOT FROM THE ISRAELIS.

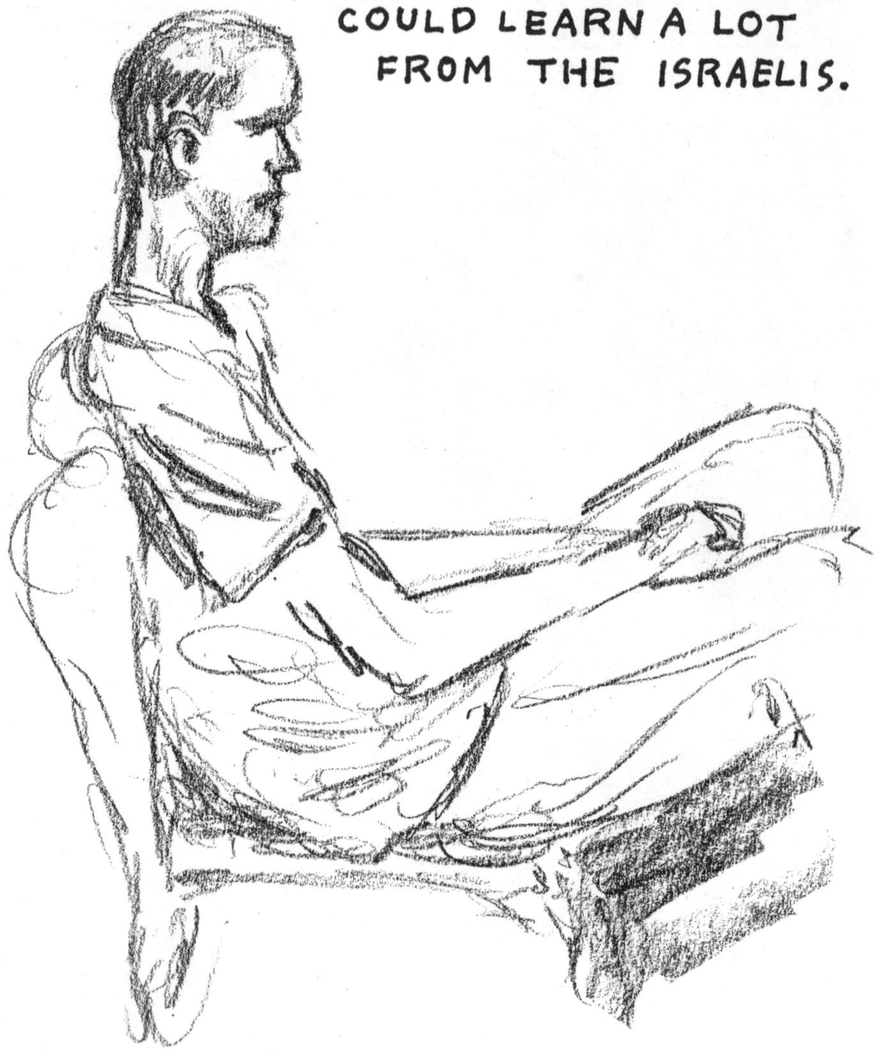

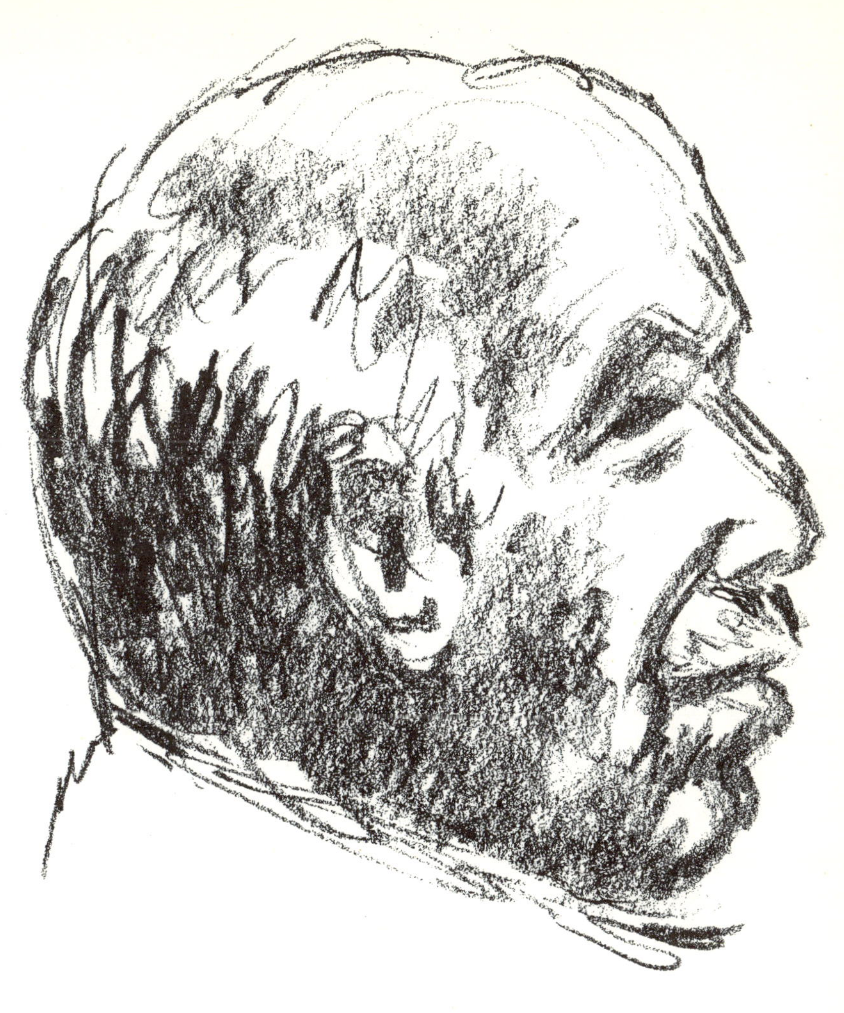

THIS MAN WAS VERY
FRIENDLY. HE GAVE
ME DIRECTIONS.

TEACHING AND LEARNING FROM THE CHILDREN of DIR IBZIA

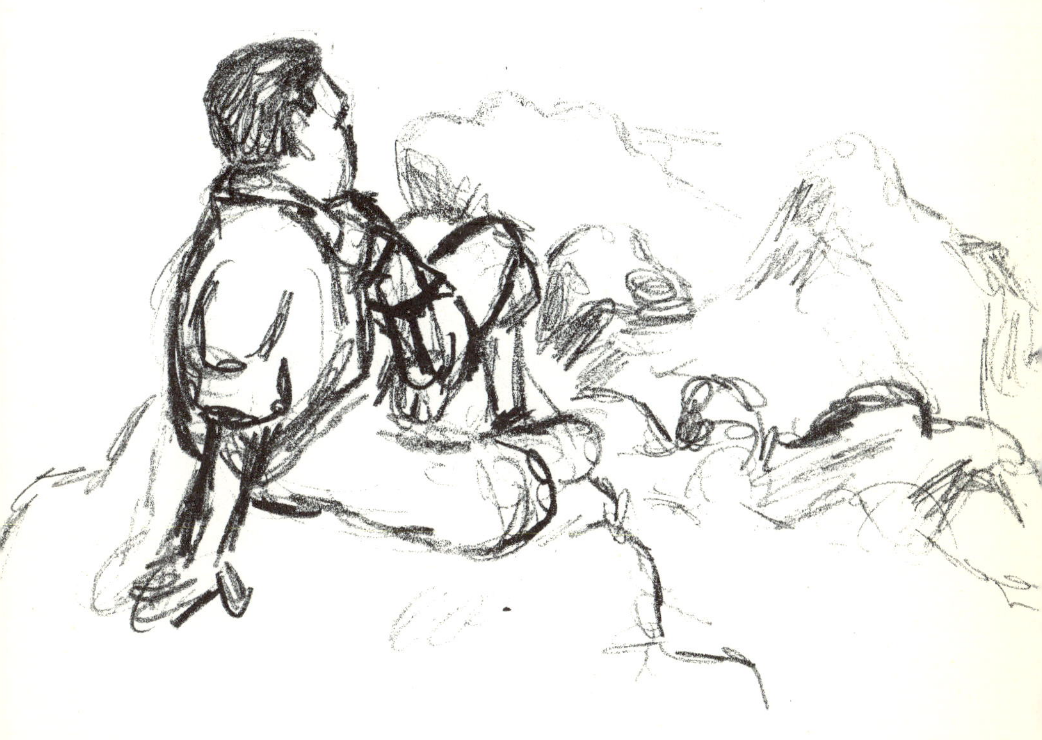

DEEB KAMAL

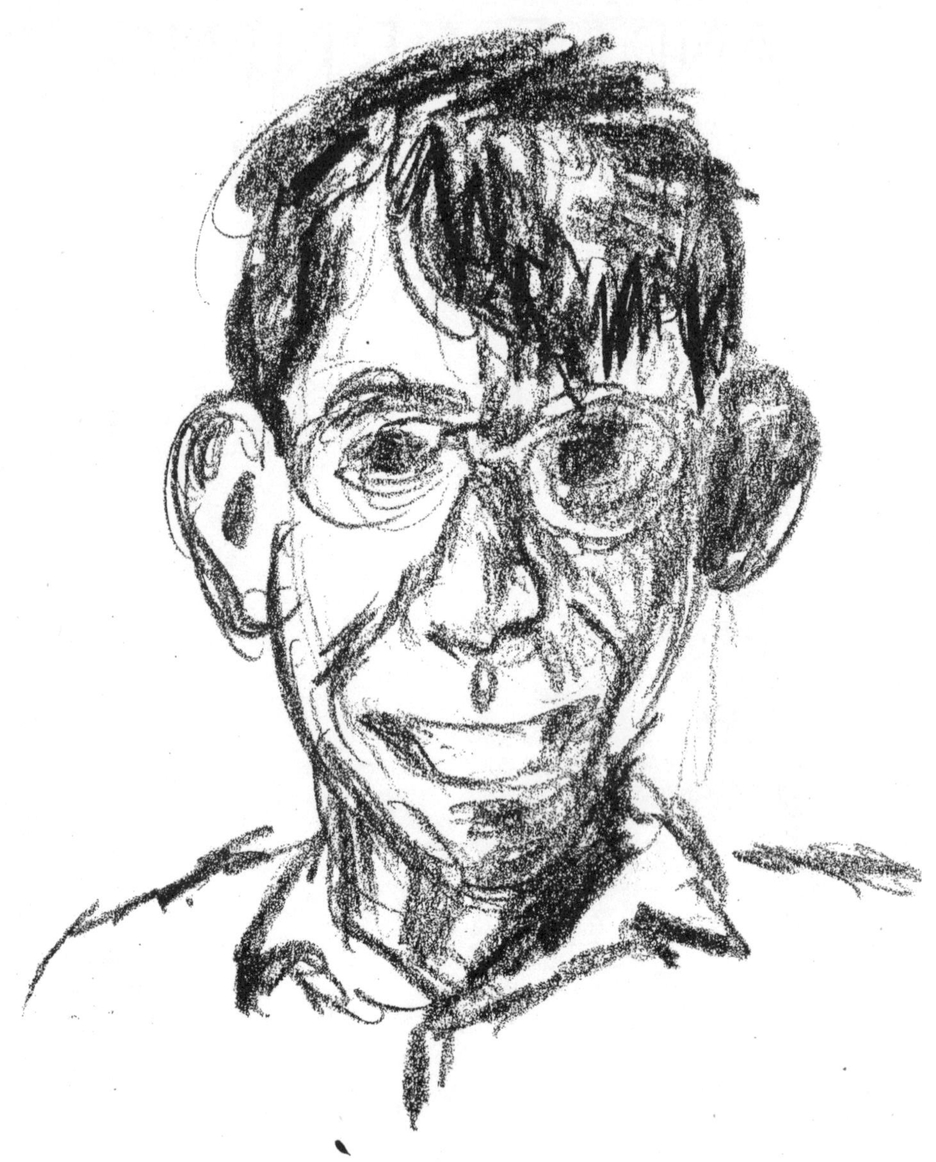

ORGANIZED
THE SUMMER SCHOOL
IN DIR IBZIA

DEEB KAMAL WAS BORN IN DIR IBZIA BUT HIS FAMLY MOVED TO JORDAN WHEN HE WAS STILL YOUNG. HE SERVED IN THE JORDANIAN ARMY, THEN MOVED TO EUROPE WHERE HE STARTED AN AUTO-PARTS BUSINESS. AFTER OSLO HE MOVED BACK TO DIRIBZIA, HOPING TO HELP BUILD THE PROMISED PALESTINIAN STATE. DEEB STARTED A FACTORY MAKING HAND BAGS, BUT BECAUSE ISRAEL CONTROLS THE BORDERS OF PALESTINE, HE WAS NOT ALLOWED TO EXPORT THE BAGS. HE HAD TO SELL THEM TO AN ISRAELI COMPANY FOR A SMALL PRICE. THEY THEN WOULD TURN AROUND AND SELL THE BAGS FOR A MUCH HIGHER PRICE. HE DECIDED THERE WAS NO POINT IN TRYING TO MAKE MONEY 'TIL PALESTINE WAS AN INDEPENDENT STATE. HE NOW DEVOTES HIS TIME TO EDUCATING THE YOUNG.

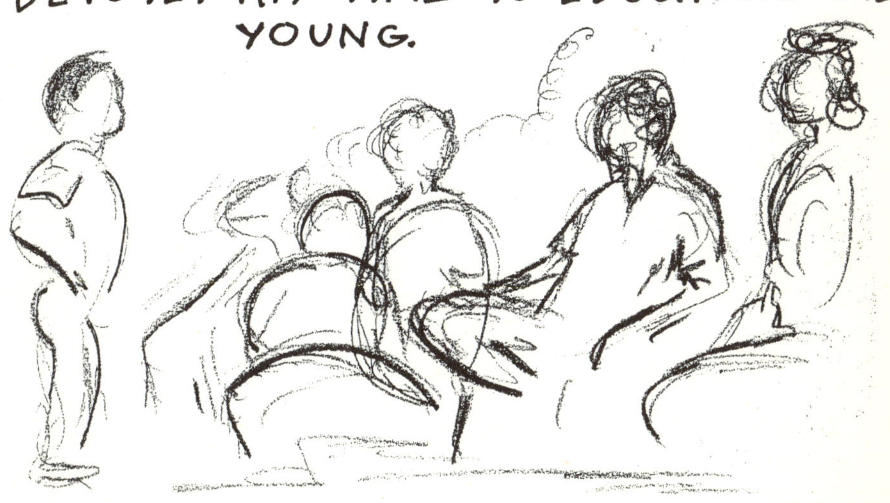

BECAUSE DEEB'S HOUSE WAS ON TOP OF A HILL, THE ARMY OFTEN WOULD TAKE IT OVER WHEN THEY INVADED THE TOWN. SO DEEB'S SON, FERAS, GREW UP WATCHING SOLDIERS HOLDING HIS PARENTS AT GUNPOINT.

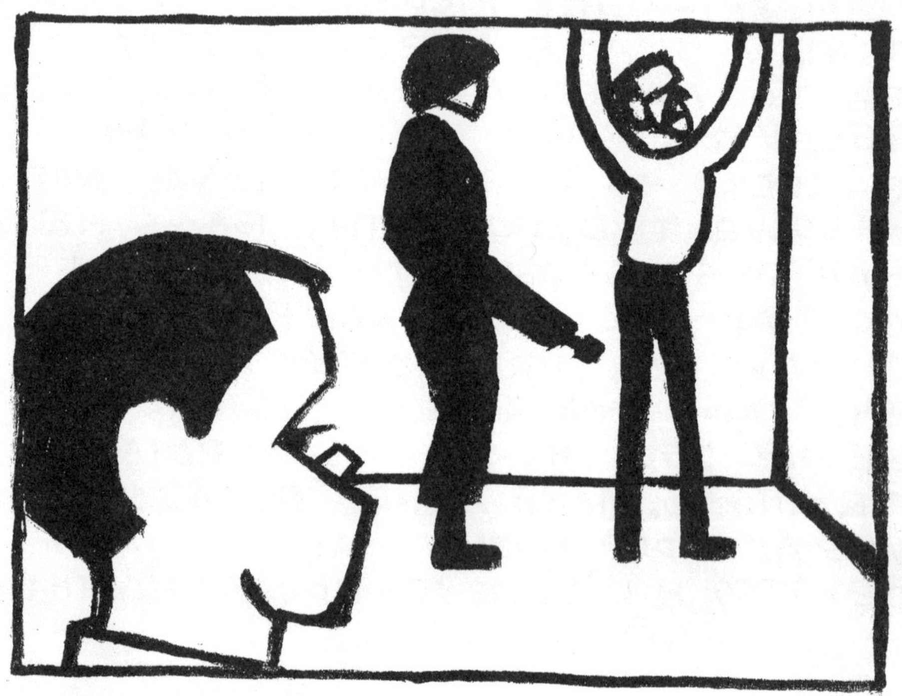

ONE DAY DEEB CAUGHT HIS SON TELLING HIS PLAYMATES THAT HIS GRANDFATHER HAD BEEN KILLED BY THE ARMY.

"THIS IS **NOT** HOW HE DIED." SAYS DEEB, "THAT IS WHEN I BEGIN TO THINK OUR VILLAGE NEEDS A CHILD PSYCHOLOGIST."

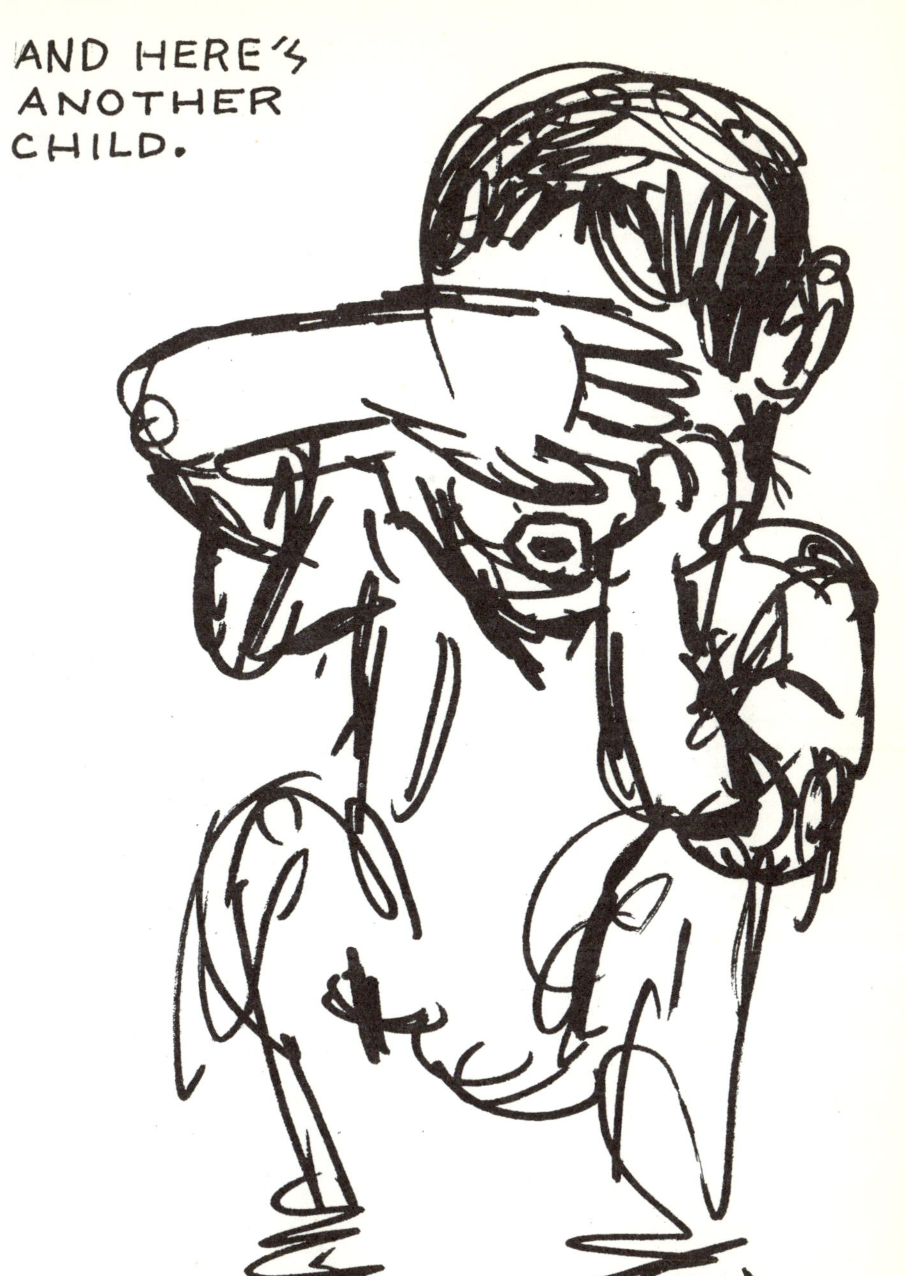

THIS BOY BECAME SCARED ANY TIME A NON-ARAB WAS IN THE ROOM. HIS FATHER NAMED HIM GANDHI.

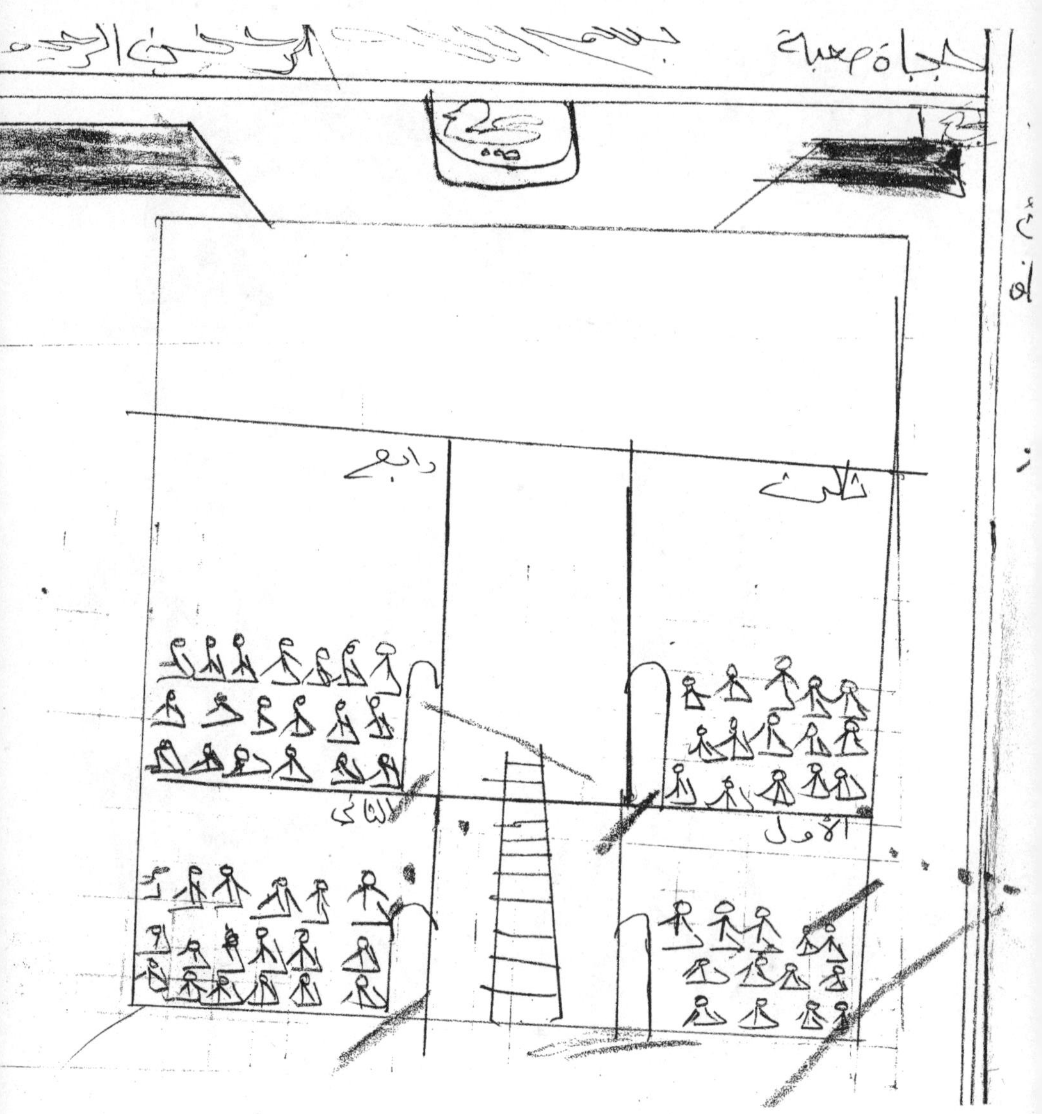

This child's drawing tells the true story of a tank firing tear GAS into a school house in Dir Ibzia. Villagers asked the soldiers why they would gas children. The soldiers replied, "We were frightened of those children."

"He was just a child like any other, going to school. When he got to school the occupying forces started bombing. Birds were flying in the early morning hours looking for something to eat or drink. The occupying forces killed them.

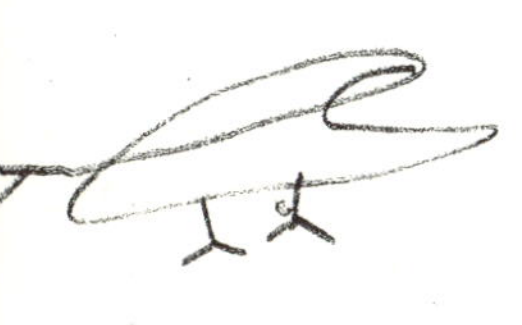

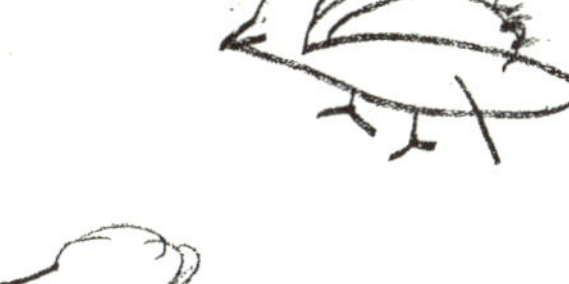

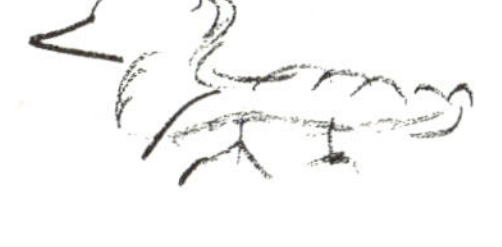

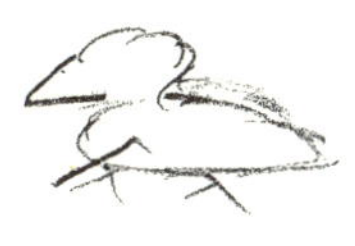

Fear and terror were all over but life goes on."

by: Ali Jawan

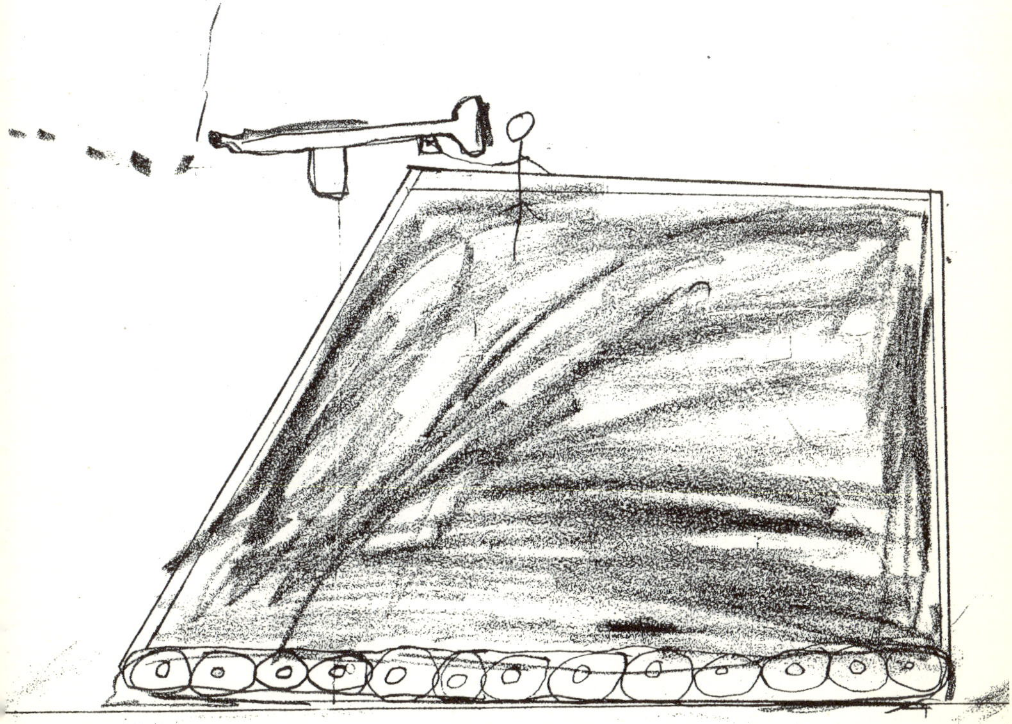

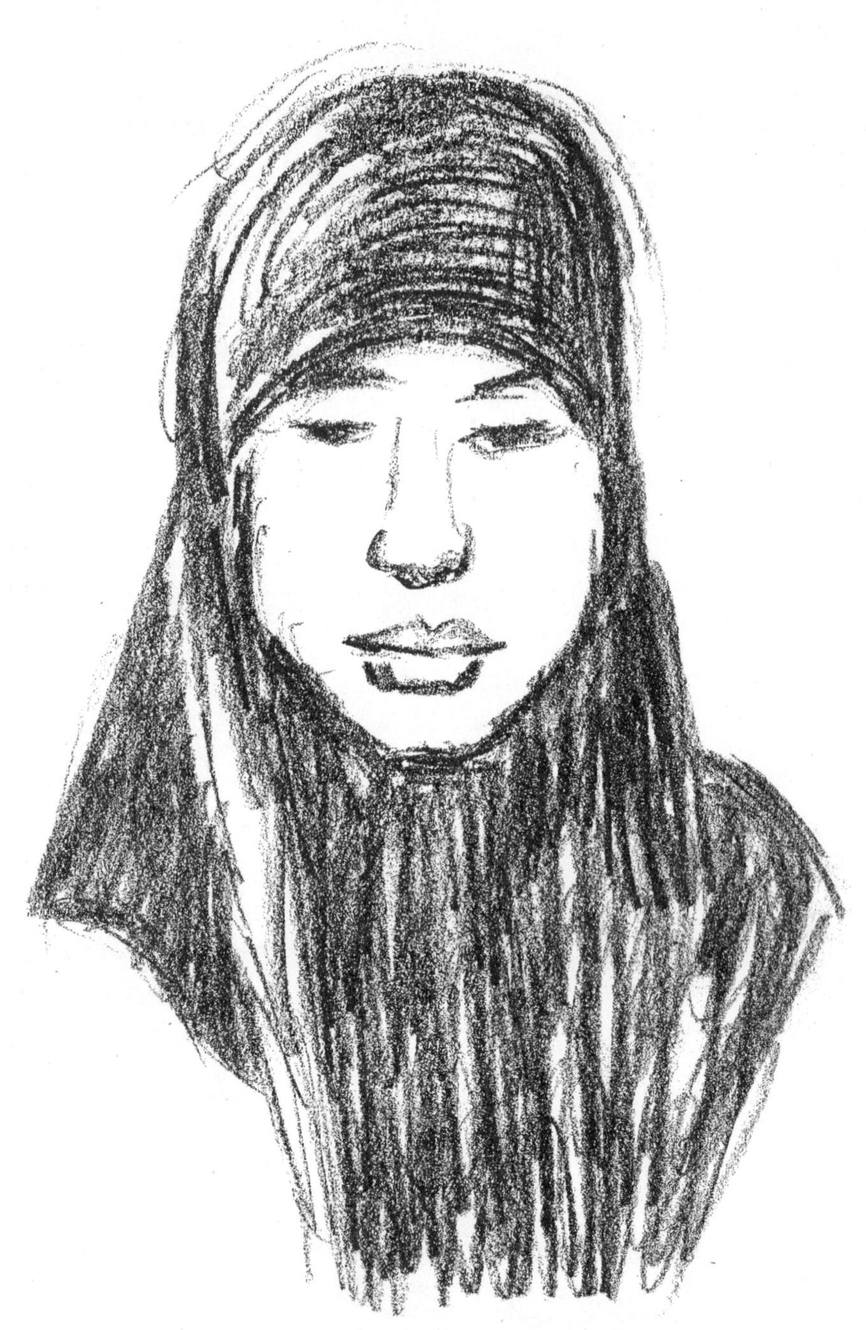

THIS 13-YEAR OLD GIRL
HAS NO FATHER.

HER NAME IS
INTEFADA MAHMED SALEEM.

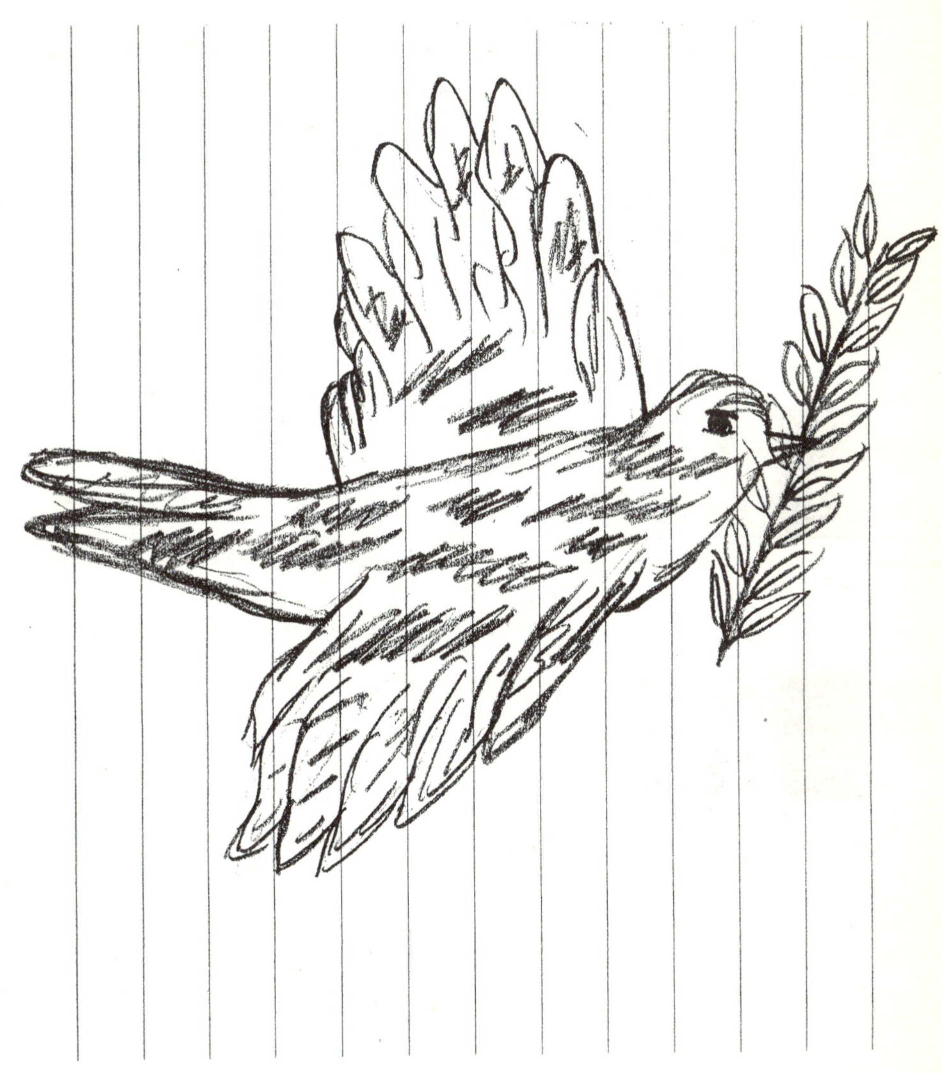

SHE DREW
THIS PICTURE.

"IF YOU WANT TO UNDERSTAND THESE CHILDREN, MAYBE I CAN ENLIGHTEN YOU. IT WASN'T SO LONG AGO WHEN I WAS ONE OF THEM. WHEN I AM A CHILD, I CAN SAY NOTHING IN MY FATHER'S HOUSE. I AM CHILD! ONLY MY FATHER CAN SPEAK! WHEN I AM IN SCHOOL, THE PART OF THE BIOLOGY BOOK WHICH IS ABOUT THE HUMAN BODY, THEY SAY IS NOT GOOD TO READ. I AM NOT ALLOWED TO KNOW ANYTHING ABOUT MY OWN BODY."

"THEN ONE DAY I AM PLAYING IN THE STREET. I HAVE SHIRT WITH THE PALESTINIAN FLAG. A SOLDIER STOPS ME. HE SAYS "DO YOU LIKE THAT FLAG?" I SAY "YES, I LIKE IT." HE SAYS "WHY DO YOU LIKE THAT FLAG?" I SAY "IT IS FLAG OF MY COUNTRY." HE SAYS "YOU SEE THE FLAG ON THAT BUILDING? I WANT YOU TO GO TAKE IT DOWN." I SAY "I CAN'T DO THAT." SO HE RIPS MY SHIRT. WHEN I GET HOME, MY FATHER SAYS "YOU ARE MESSING AROUND IN THE STREET AND RUIN YOUR CLOTHES." HE STARTS TO BEAT ME. I TELL MY MOM WHAT HAPPENED, BUT HE WON'T BELIEVE HER. THAT IS WHEN I REALIZE I AM REALLY IN TROUBLE, BECAUSE I AM NOT JUST UNDER OCCUPATION. I AM UNDER TWO OCCUPATIONS."

MAZEED

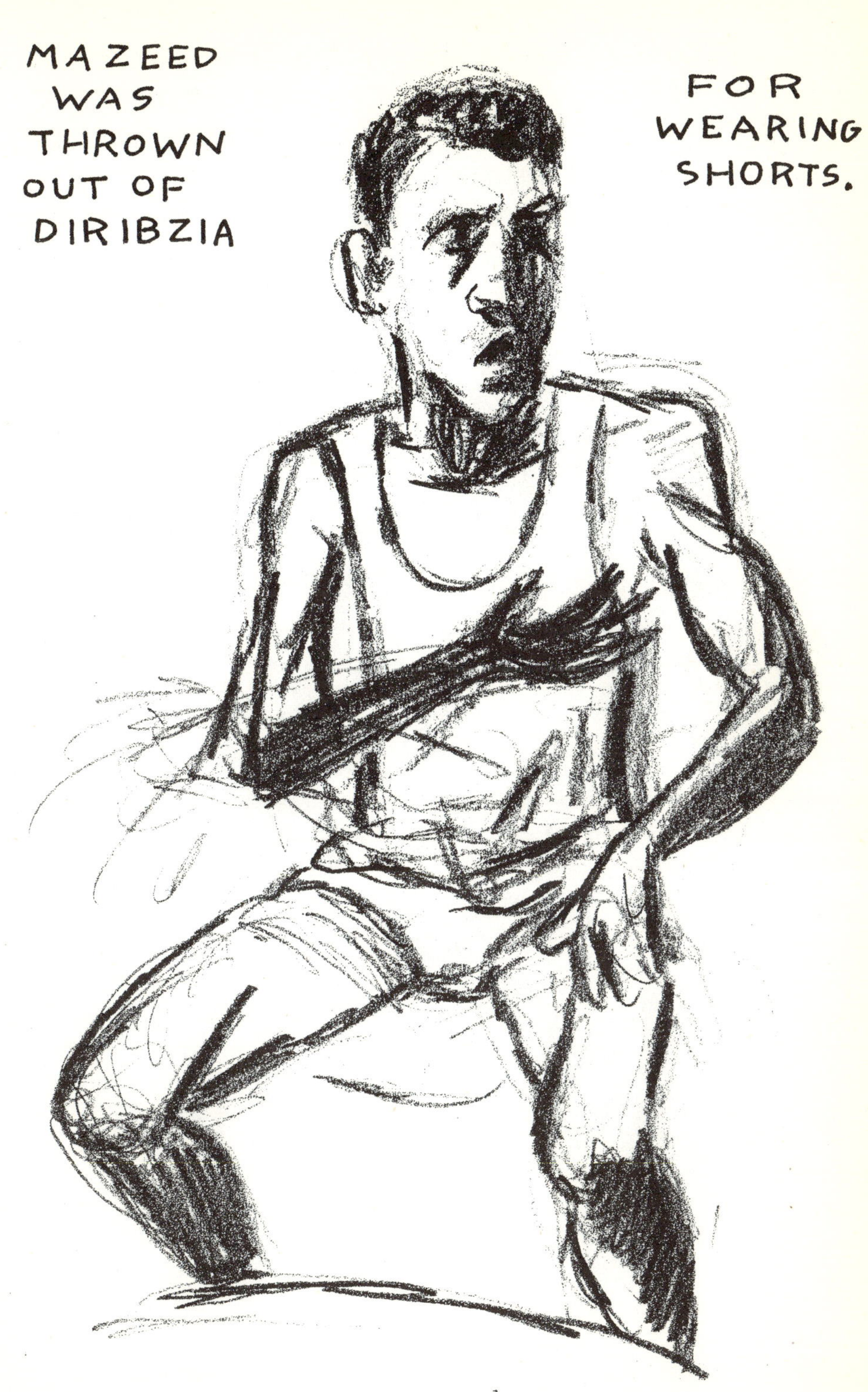
MAZEED WAS THROWN OUT OF DIRIBZIA
FOR WEARING SHORTS.

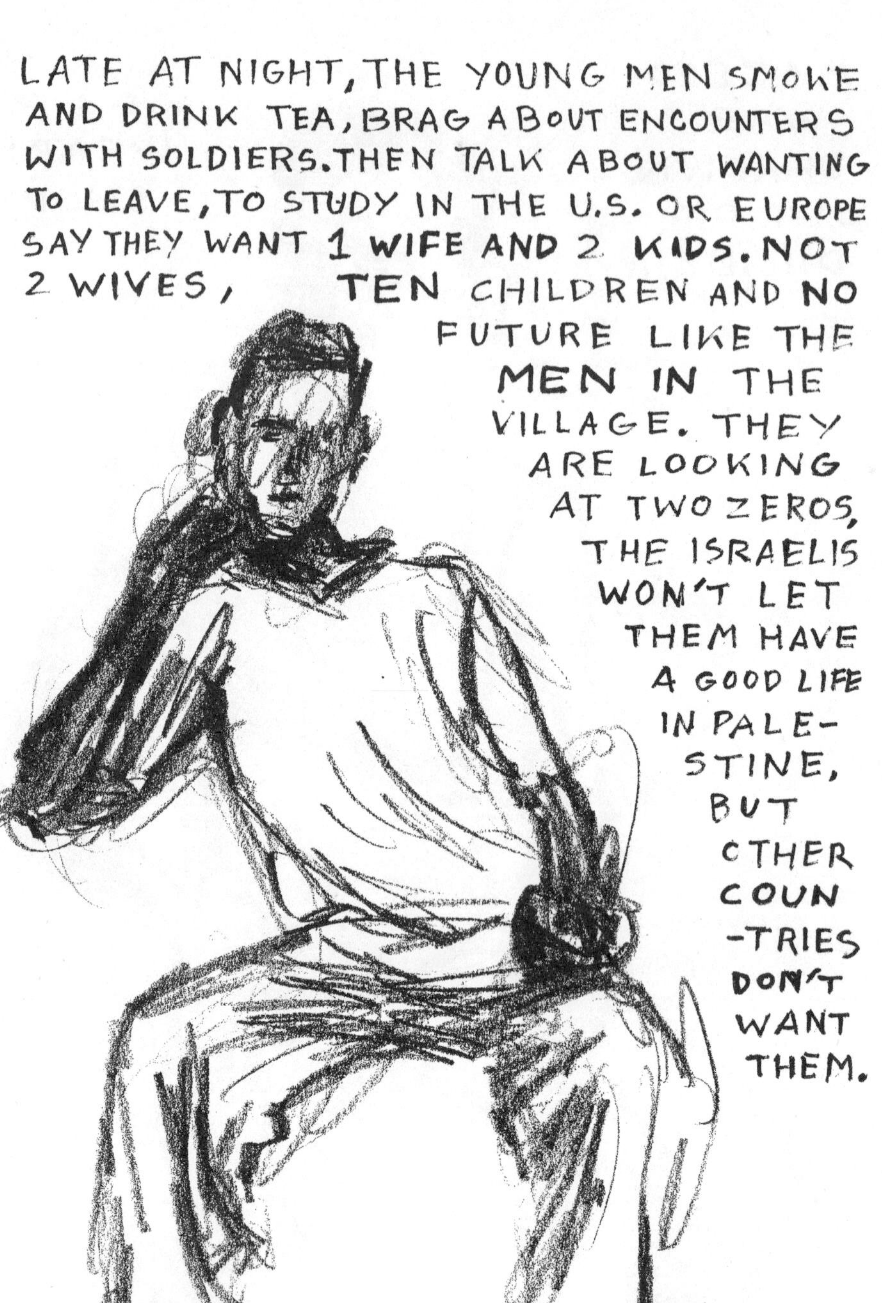
LATE AT NIGHT, THE YOUNG MEN SMOKE AND DRINK TEA, BRAG ABOUT ENCOUNTERS WITH SOLDIERS. THEN TALK ABOUT WANTING TO LEAVE, TO STUDY IN THE U.S. OR EUROPE SAY THEY WANT 1 WIFE AND 2 KIDS. NOT 2 WIVES, TEN CHILDREN AND NO FUTURE LIKE THE MEN IN THE VILLAGE. THEY ARE LOOKING AT TWO ZEROS, THE ISRAELIS WON'T LET THEM HAVE A GOOD LIFE IN PALE-STINE, BUT OTHER COUN-TRIES DON'T WANT THEM.

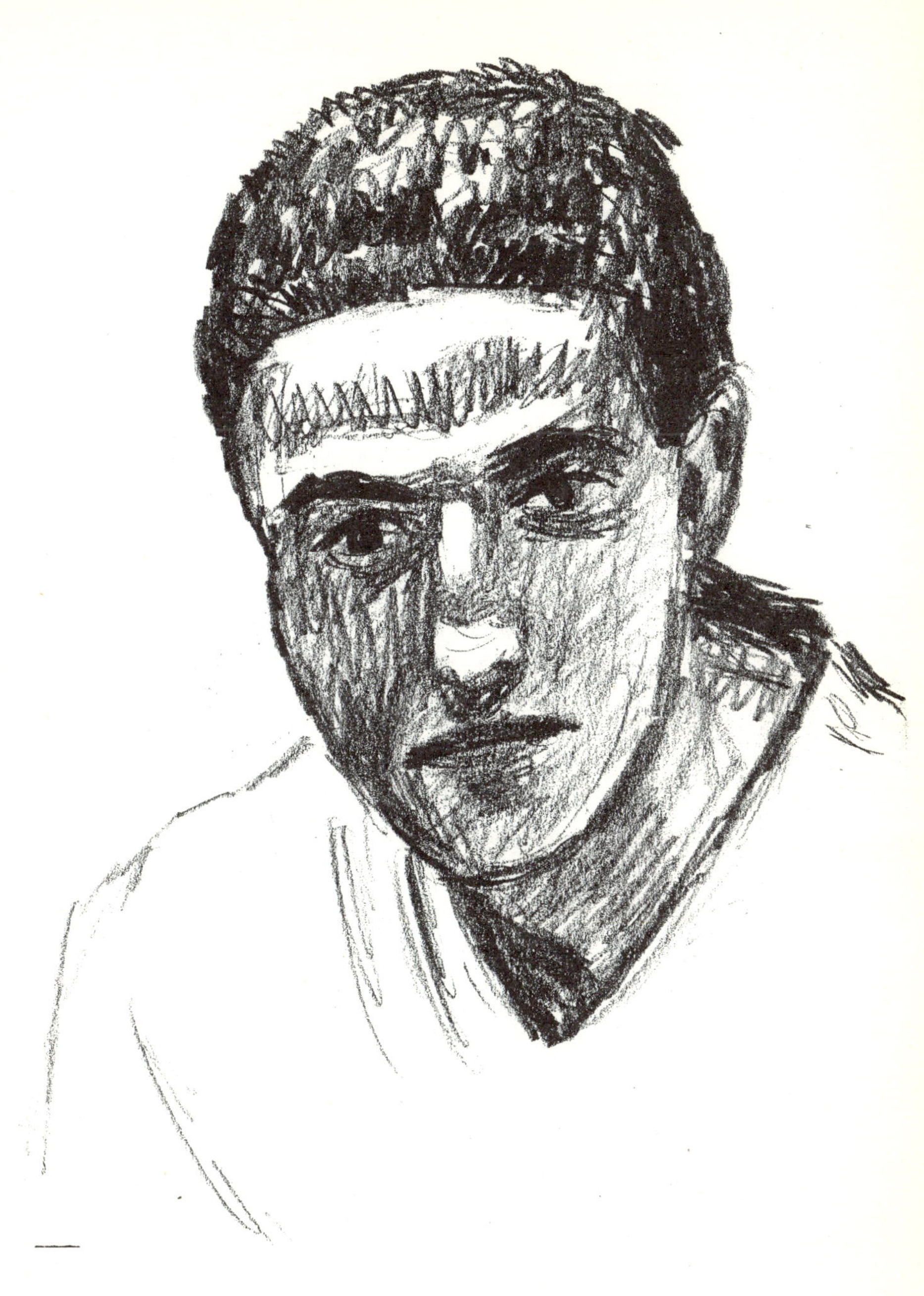

MR. HASSAN WORKS FOR THE PALESTINIAN AUTHORITY IN THE DEPARTMENT OF AGRICULTURE. BUT BECAUSE OF THE SITUATION THERE IS LITTLE WORK FOR HIM TO DO. SO MR. HASSAN BEGAN TO WORK WITH US AT THE SCHOOL PART TIME, TEACHING THE KIDS ABOUT ECOLOGY. AFTER THE FIRST WEEK OF SCHOOL THE ISRAELIS BEGAN LIFTING THE CURFEW IN RAMALLAH FOR A FEW HOURS A DAY. THE P.A. FOUND OUT THAT MR. HASSAN WAS MOONLIGHTING. HE WAS ORDERED TO STOP TEACHING BECAUSE THE SCHOOL WAS NOT A P.A. PROJECT. SOME PEOPLE IN THE VILLAGE SAY THE P.A. AND HAMAS JUST FUNNEL AID MONEY TO THEIR SUPPORTERS AND DONT DO ANYTHING FOR THE AVERAGE PERSON.

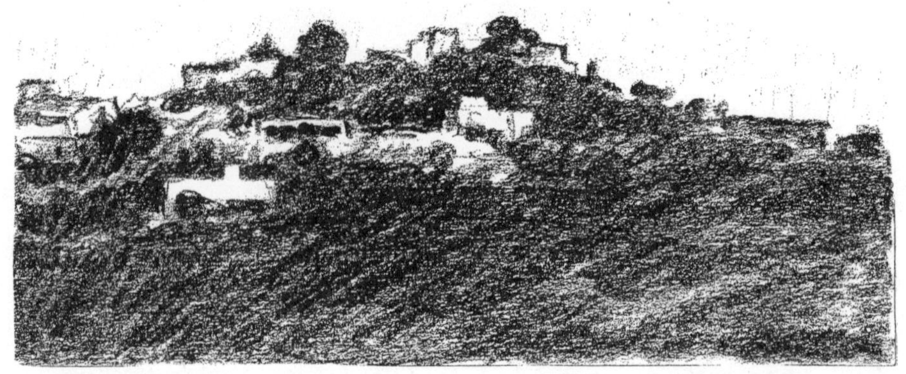

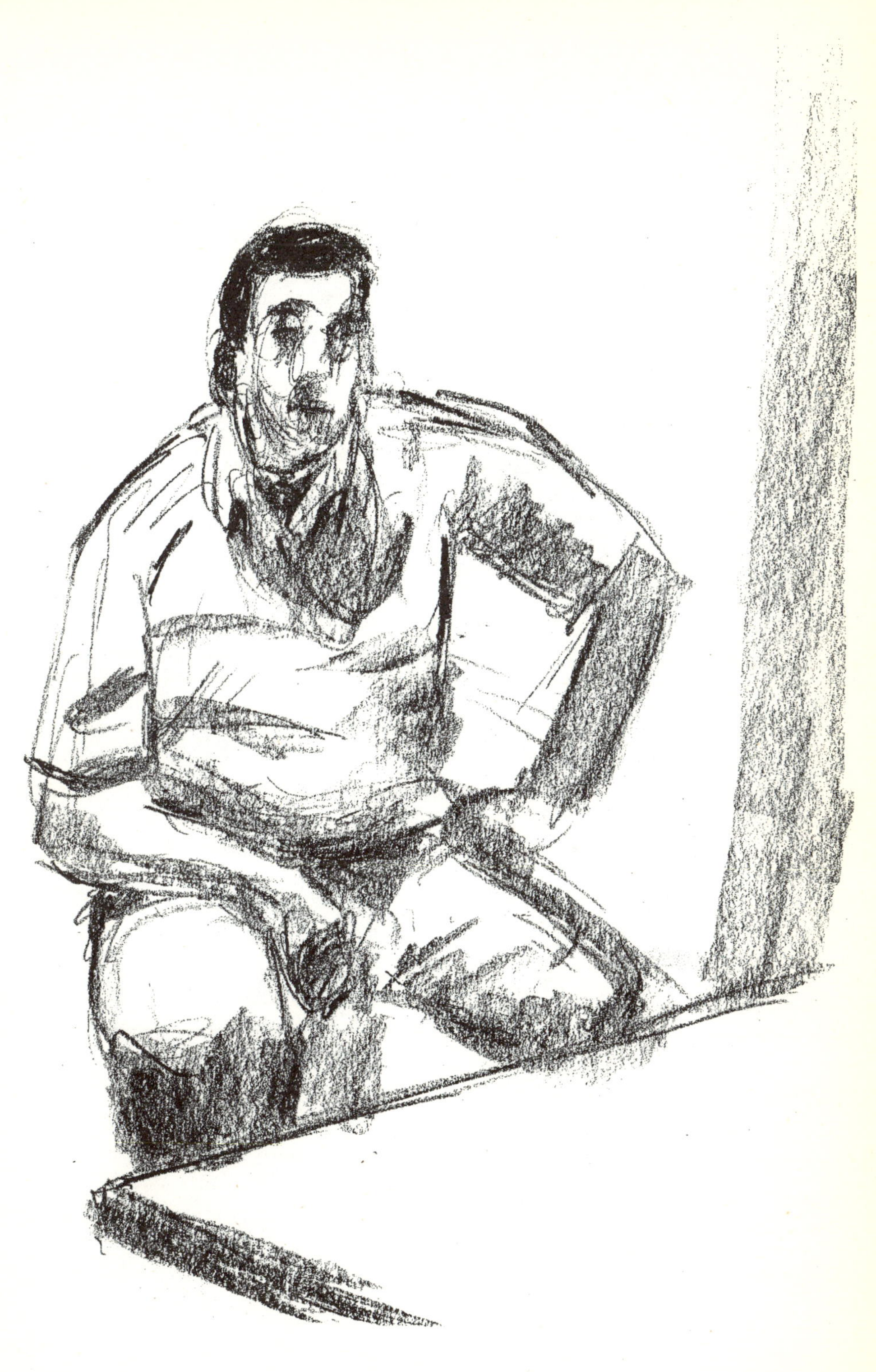

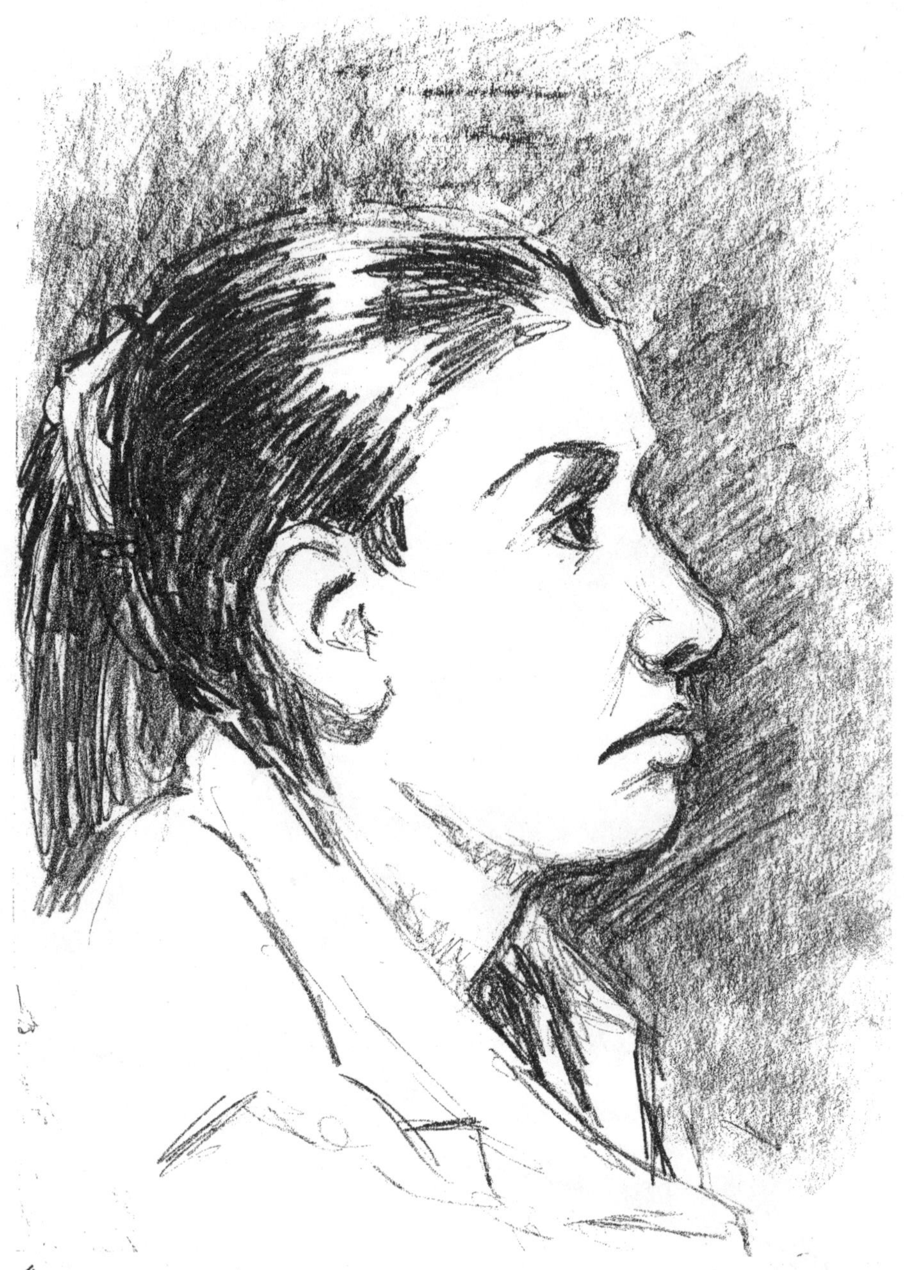

"MY SISTER LEILA HAD TO GO BACK TO SCHOOL MONDAY, AND THEN RAMALLAH WAS CLOSED YESTERDAY BECAUSE THE ISRAELIS KILLED SOMEONE AND THEY DIDN'T WANT PEOPLE MAKING A DEMONSTRATION DURING THE FUNERAL....NOTHING CHANGES HERE, WE CANT EVEN PLAN TO GO TO SCHOOL TOMORROW!"

NADIA KAMAL

IT'S OFTEN SAID THAT "THE ARABS ARE TEACHING THEIR CHILDREN TO HATE." THE FOLKS I MET JUST WANTED THEIR KIDS TO LEARN ENGLISH SO THEY COULD GET BETTER JOBS.

THE BIRTHRIGHT PROGRAM WILL PAY THE EXPENSES OF ANY YOUNG AMERICAN JEW WHO WANTS TO VISIT ISRAEL. THEY OFFER A FREE GUIDED TOUR OF HOLY SITES, BEACHES AND DISCOS. A LOT OF $ IS BEING SPENT TO MAKE SURE AMERICAN JEWS LOVE ISRAEL. BUT AMERICAN JEWS CAN'T GIVE ISRAEL PEACE. WHAT IS BEING DONE FOR THE KIDS IN THE WEST BANK?

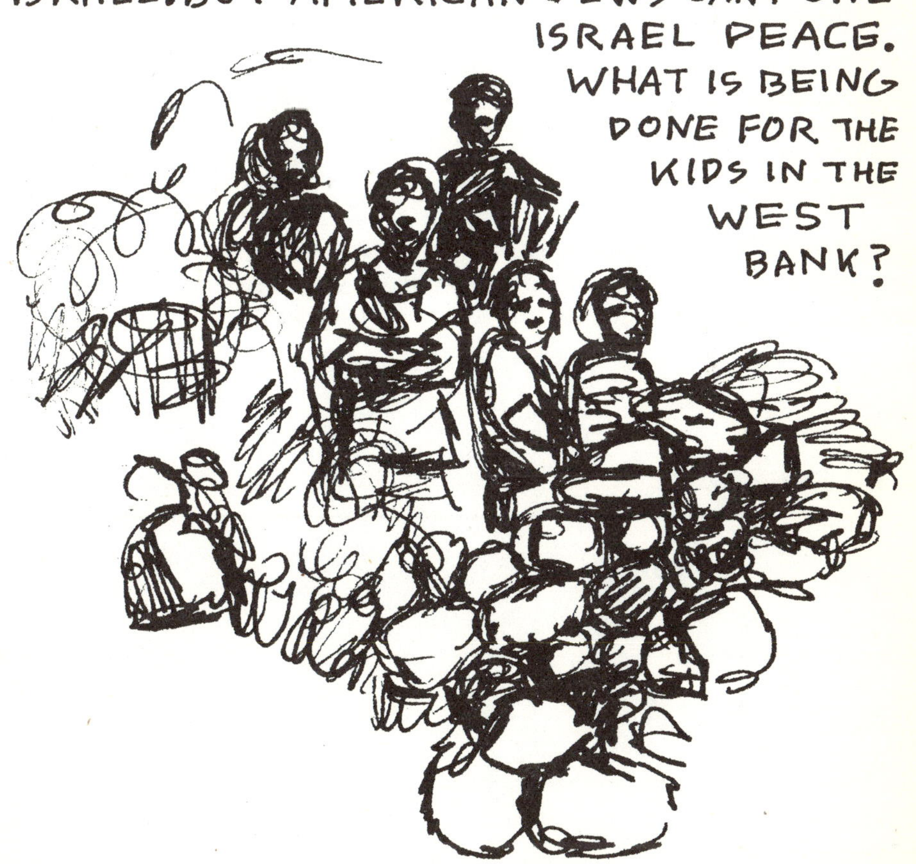

INTER-

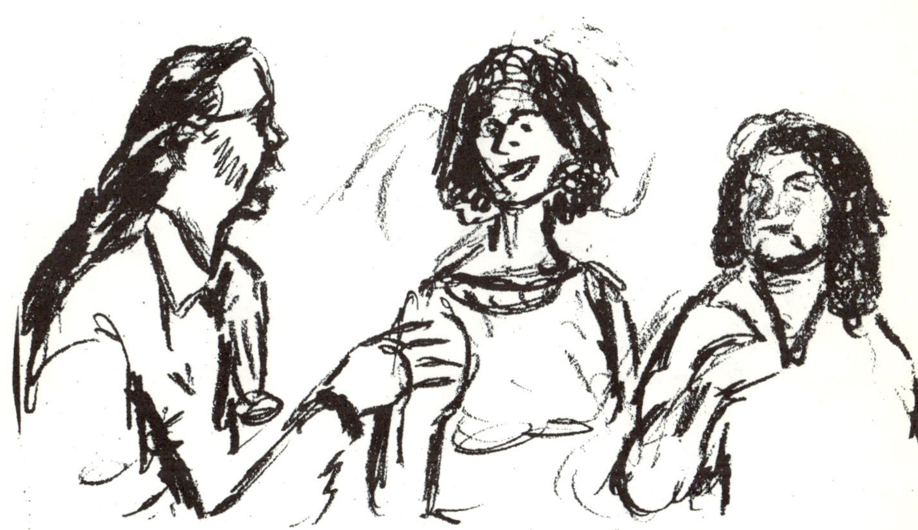

NATIONALS

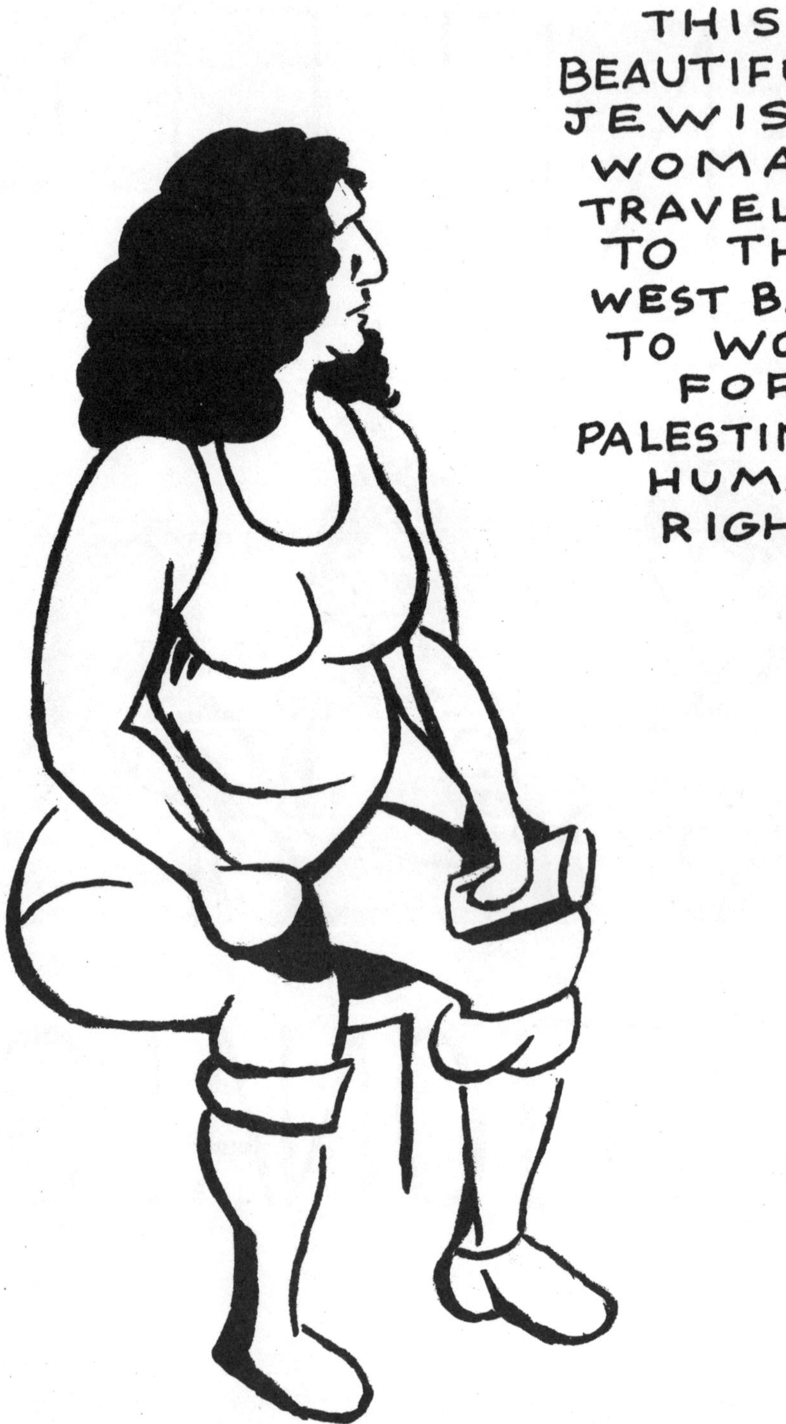
THIS BEAUTIFUL JEWISH WOMAN TRAVELED TO THE WEST BANK TO WORK FOR PALESTINIAN HUMAN RIGHTS.

AND THIS EUROPEAN ARAB, ALSO CAME TO THE MIDDLE EAST TO HELP THE PALESTINIANS, THROUGH NONVIOLENT DIRECT ACTION.

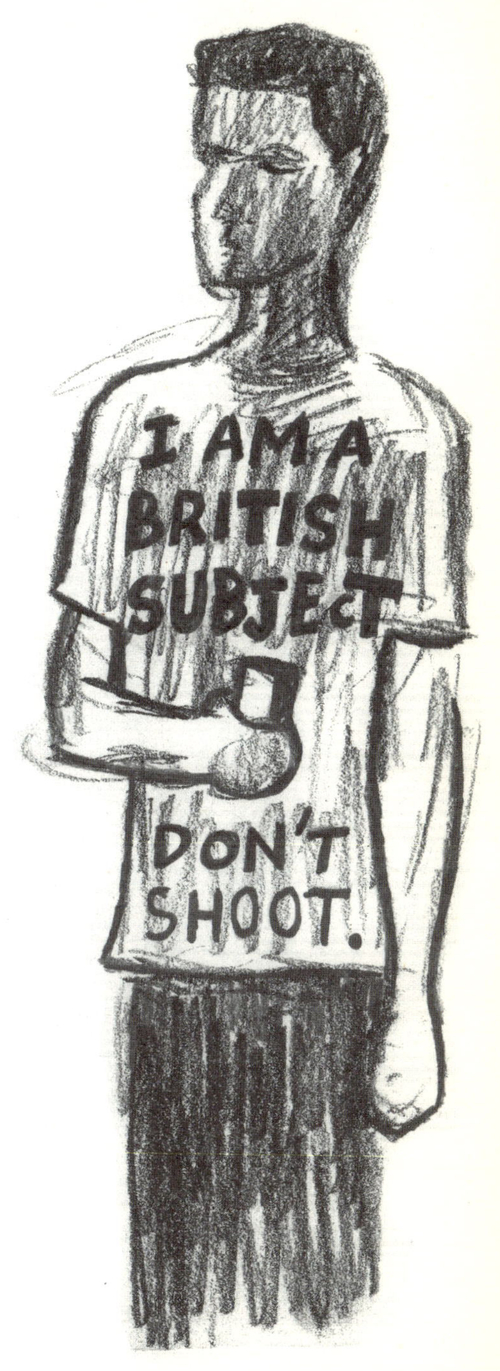

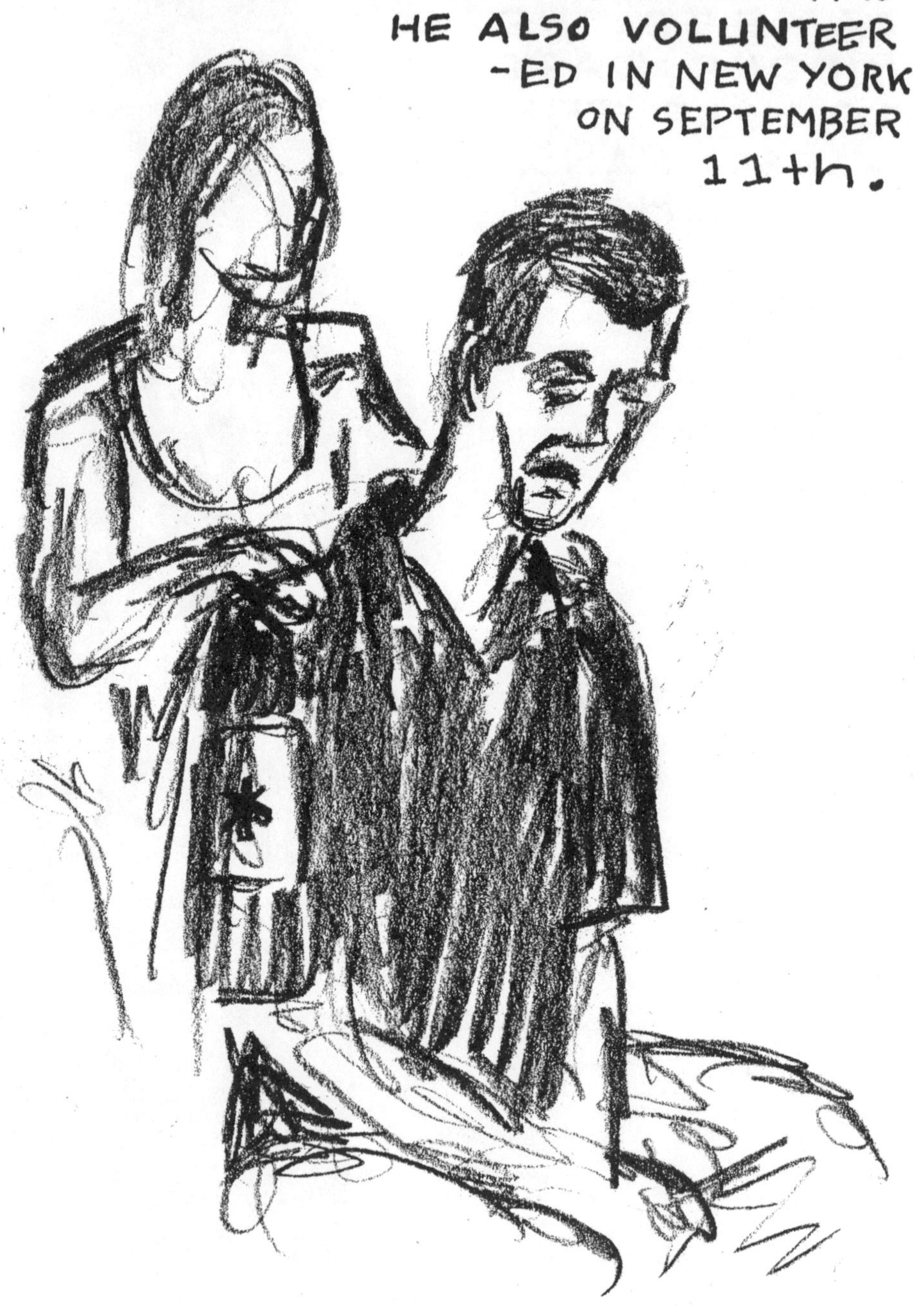
THIS AMERICAN AMBULANCE DRIVER HAS JUST COME BACK FROM VOLUNTEERING IN RAMALLAH.
HE ALSO VOLUNTEER-ED IN NEW YORK ON SEPTEMBER 11th.

"ONE OF THE THINGS THAT REALLY DROVE ME TO BECOME ACTIVE WAS SEEING JEWISH ACTIVISTS GET INVOLVED. IT WAS A HOPEFUL PROSPECT.

BUT NOW I THINK IT'S PRETTY MUCH IRRELEVENT. PALESTINIAN LIBERATION IS AN ISSUE OF UNIVERSAL SOCIAL JUSTICE. WHAT REALLY MATTERS IS THAT INDIVIDUALS ACT TOGETHER UNDER A FRAMEWORK OF ELEMENTARY MORAL PRINCIPALS, NOT THE ETHNIC MAKE UP OF THE ACTIVISTS."

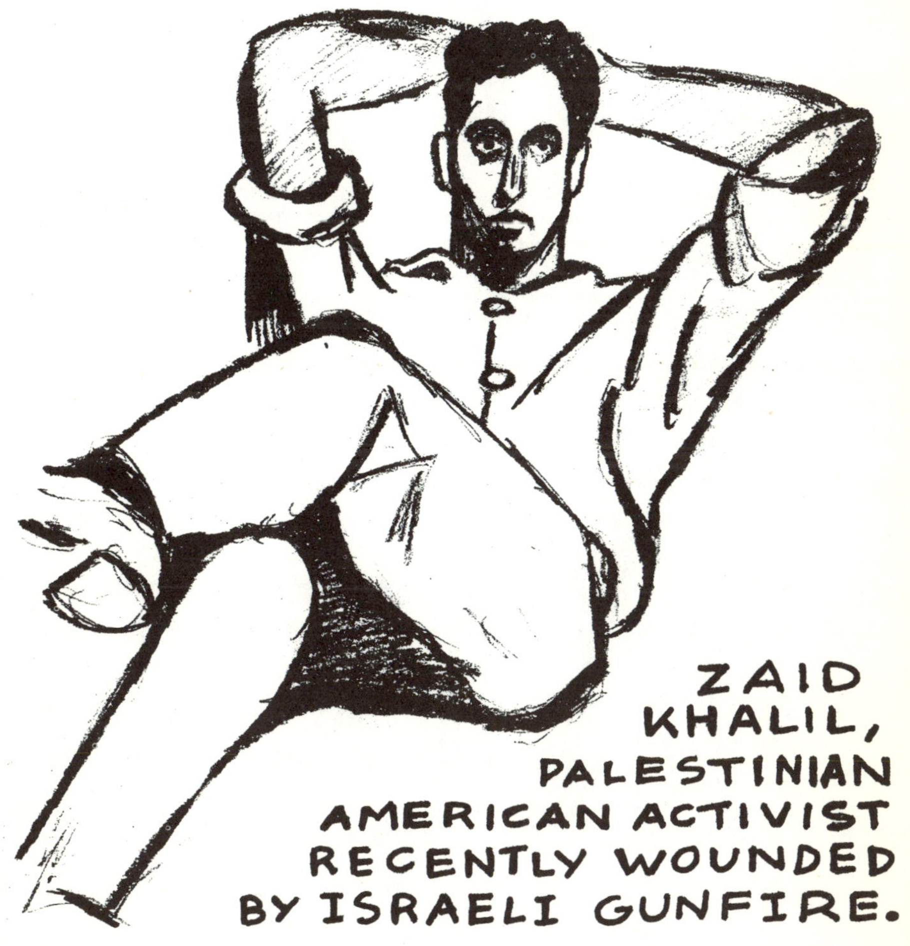

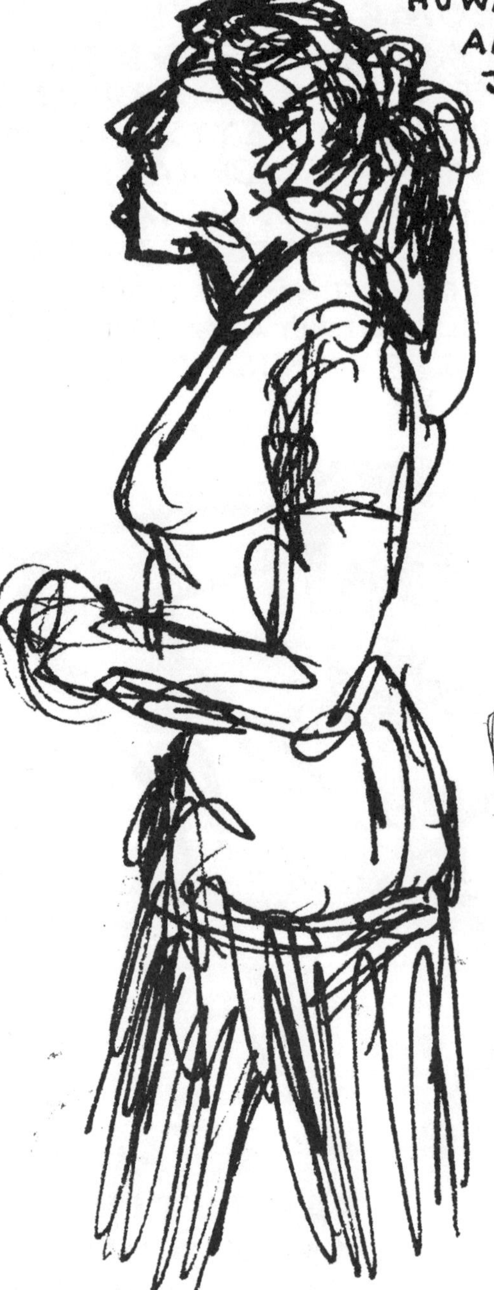

HUWAIDA IS PALESTINIAN AMERICAN. ADAM IS A JEW FROM NEW YORK. THEY ARE MARRIED.

THEY ORGANIZE NONVIOLENT RESISTANCE TO THE OCCUPATION. THE PAPERS CALL ADAM THE "JEWISH TALIBAN". FROM WHAT THE PAPERS SAY, YOU WOULD EXPECT HIM TO HAVE HORNS AND A TAIL.

BUT IF YOU LISTEN TO WHAT ADAM SAYS, HE TURNS OUT TO BE VERY REASONABLE. IN THIS RESPECT, HE RESEMBLES EVERY REAL CIVIL RIGHTS LEADER I HAVE EVER MET. HERE IS ADAM SPEAKING IN NEW YORK.

"WE ARE NOT ASKING YOU TO CHANGE YOUR OPINION. SUPPORT ISRAEL. SUPPORT A STRONG ISRAEL. BUT SUPPORT ISRAEL WITHIN ITS BORDERS. SUPPORT AN ISRAEL THAT IS NOT AN OPPRESSOR. SUPPORT AN ISRAEL THAT IS PART OF THE INTERNATIONAL COMMUNITY AND RESPECTS INTERNATIONAL LAW. SUPPORT ISRAEL AND AS JEWISH PEOPLE STAND UP FOR FREEDOM."

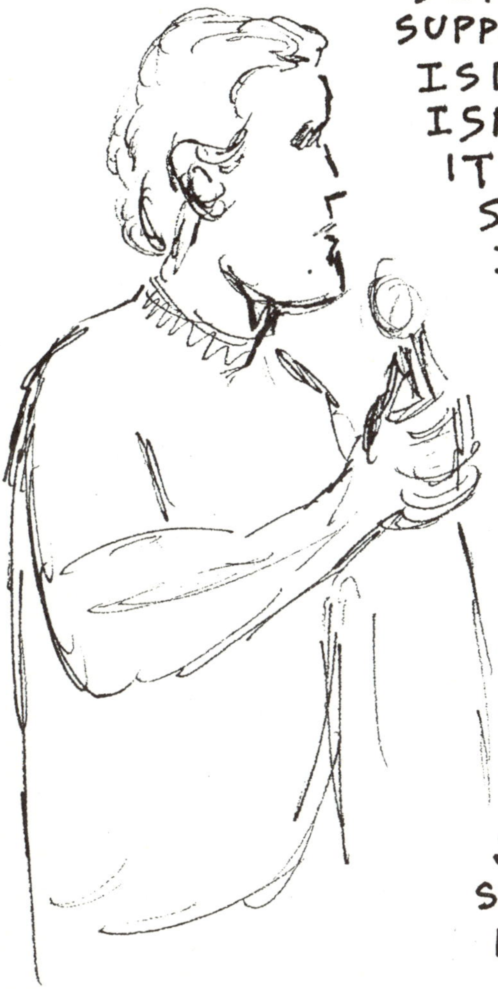

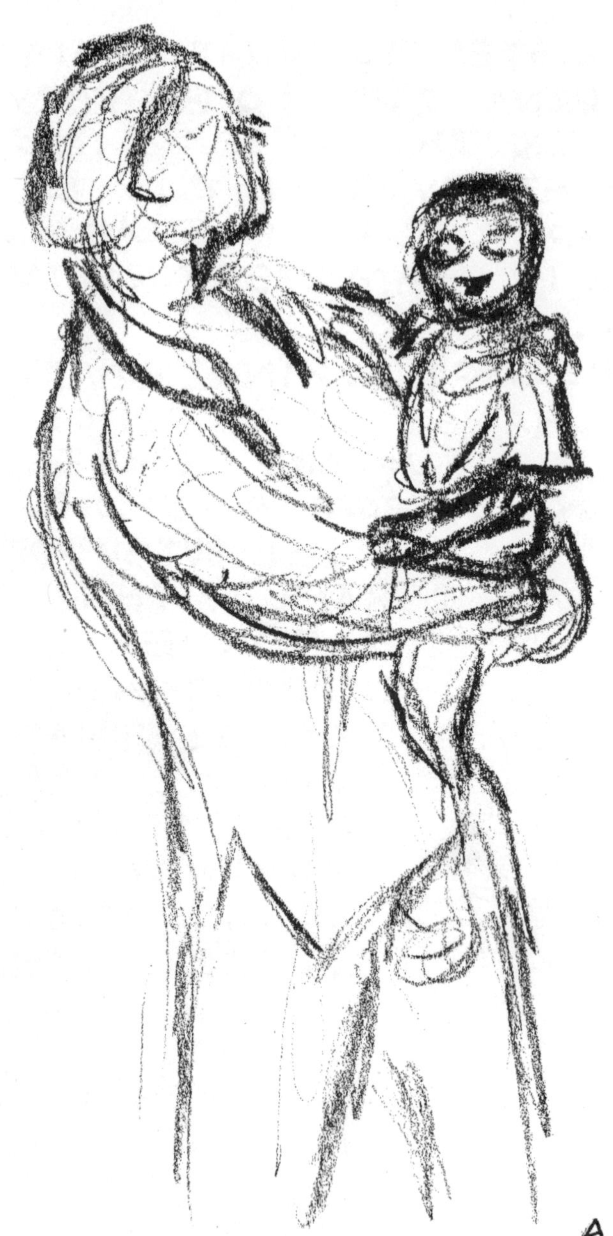

A JEWISH
-AMERICAN
WOMAN SINGING TO A
PALESTINIAN CHILD IN THE
HOSPITAL IN RAMALLAH.